Poor Will's

Almanack

for 2017

by

Bill Felker

The sun rises and the sun goes down and hurries to the place where it rises. The wind blows to the south and goes around to the north; round and round goes the wind, And on its circuits the wind return.

Quoheleth

Bill Felker

ISBN-13: 9781453787090

TABLE OF CONTENTS

Part I:
Introductions to:

Part II:
An Overview of the Forty-Eight Seasons of the Year

Part III:
The Monthly Almanack Entries
Which Contain:

Seasonal Quotation
Gregorian Calendar
Essay by Bill Felker
The Names and Phases of the Moon
The Seasonal Affective Disorder Index
Notes on the Sun's Position, the Position of Major
Planets, the Stars and the Shooting Stars
A Calendar of Feast Days and Holidays
Farming and Gardening with the Moon
The Moon and the Weather
Phenology: When...Then
Calendar of Blooming Plants
Peak Activity Times for Creatures
Almanack Literature: A Reader Story

Part I
Introductions

The Dominical Forecast for 2017

During the Middle Ages, the letters A through G were sometimes assigned to the first Sunday of the New Year. If that Sunday fell on January 1, then that Sunday's letter (or "Dominical" Letter) was A. If the first Sunday of the year fell on January 2, the dominical letter was B, and so forth.

Using Dominical Letters as the basis for forecasting weather and fortune, Robert Reynes, overseer of the village of Acle in Norfolk, England, formulated prognostications for each dominical situation in his *Yeoman's Commonplace Book*, which he wrote between 1470 and 1475.

This year the first Sunday falls on January 1; therefore, the Dominical letter for the year is A, and Reynes' forecast is the following:

"When the Dominical letter falls on the A, then there shall be a warm winter and a stormy summer, grain in the field, but just a reasonable amount of fruit; in the same way there shall be pestilence among young people and death of beasts, especially of cattle; great conflict and fighting among robbers and new tidings of kings."

Although many centuries have passed since Reynes developed his system, it may actually be as useful as other forms of predicting the future.

Certainly, given the current trends of climate change (increasing heat and more extreme weather events), a warm winter and a stormy summer are actually quite probable.

Grain in the field and a reasonable amount of fruit? It seems that such conditions might occur, provided that the warm winter and storms of summer don't spoil everything.

As for pestilence among young people, one can choose among the Zika virus, suicide, murder, car accidents and heroin. And the death of beasts is also a fair prediction, considering that 2017 lies in the middle of the Sixth Great Extinction. Also, be on the lookout for bird flu, mad cow disease and who knows what else.

It also seems likely that the *Yeoman's Commonplace Book* will be right on the money when it comes to "great conflict and fighting among robbers," especially if that statement refers to gang violence and foreign affairs.

As for "new tidings of kings," will there be a change of leadership in the House of Representatives and the Senate during 2017? We'll have to wait and see about that.

For sure there will be new tidings of kings (or queens) in the White House.

The Weather in Poor Will's Almanack

The weather estimates in this *Almanack* are based on my charts of fractal weather patterns made between 1978 and 2016. Readers of my weekly and monthly columns throughout the United States have used these estimates successfully since 1984. For best results, readers in the East should add one to two days to specific days mentioned in the overviews. In the West, subtract one to two days.

Major high-pressure systems cross the United States an average of once every five to six days, and nearly 80 highs cross the Mississippi River in a year. Fronts move more quickly in the colder months; October through March can bring up to eight waves of high pressure every 30 days. The warmer months between April and September are more likely to have six or fewer fronts; June, July and August sometimes only produce two or three significant systems.

This regular pulse that characterizes the planet's atmosphere was first recorded in detail by 16th-century almanackers. It still forms the basis for annual predictions in today's commercial almanacks, and can be used by anyone who keeps a weather journal to gauge the likelihood for rain or sun, heat or cold on any given day.

    Poor Will's Almanack for 2017 integrates lunar conditions with descriptions of the weather systems, noting how the moon's phase and proximity to Earth could influence frontal behavior.

The Time of Day
In Poor Will's Almanack

All times in this *Almanack* are given in Eastern Standard Time.

Almanack versus Almanac

The traditional (old-fashioned) spelling (Almanack with a K) is used throughout this book.

Farming and Gardening with the Moon

    In general, planting crops that bear their fruit above the ground is recommended when the moon is waxing.

Plant root crops, flower bulbs, trees and shrubs to promote root growth when the moon is waning.

According to a number of studies, the moon exerts less influence on ocean tides and on human and animal behavior when it comes into its 2nd and 4th quarters. Therefore, it might make more sense to perform routine maintenance on your flock or herd near the date on which the moon enters its second or fourth quarter.

On the other hand, tidal lunar influences have been proven to be greater at full moon and new moon times. You might expect more trouble with your animals, therefore, on or about new moon and full moon.

Livestock care should be less eventful during the relatively stable times between frontal systems listed in each month's weather section (but before the barometer starts to drop below 30.00).

The Naming of Moons

In the United States, the naming of moons has been associated with the early inhabitants of the continent, and newcomers learned some of those names from the peoples they encountered.

Although different groups used

different names for different moons, depending on their location (and the accompanying weather and sources of food), the following list has survived as representative of what was used by some Native American nations:

January: Wolf Moon, February: Snow Moon, March: Worm Moon, April: Pink Moon, May: Flower Moon, June: Hot Moon or Strawberry Moon, July: Buck Moon, August: Sturgeon Moon, September: Harvest Moon, October: Hunter's Moon, November: Beaver Moon, December: Cold Moon.

Even though some of these names are still in use today among people who read almanacks, I believe the tradition of naming is best continued by identifying lunar times within a more personal and local context.

To some, I suppose, that might mean the creation of names like the Superbowl Moon or the World Series Moon. And such tags would certainly be more appropriate for sports fans than names of animals. Corporations might name moons for the different phases of the production and sales year. On a more intimate level, lovers might pick their moons from certain milestones in a relationship, the First Kiss Moon and so on.

My personal preference is to go to the local landscape to find some event in nature that coincides with the full moon of a particular month. In the spring and summer months, the blooming of flowers and trees provide any number of suggestions. In fall and winter, other events like leaf turn, leaf fall, migratory activity, the forcing of bulbs or the seeding of flowers and vegetables offer ample variety for selection.

The most important thing about moons or any other natural phenomenon is that we notice them, and that we take them inside ourselves and allow them to bring some balance and harmony. Among all the changes of our lives, the changes of sky and of the seasons may be the least radical and disruptive. The stability of their rhythms can offset the instability of other parts of our lives. Naming can be a reminder to take part in that gift of compensation.

The Poor Will's Almanack as Guide to Activity of Creatures

Although successful fishing is influenced primarily by the aquatic habitat, the type of bait used, the location of the bait in the water, the time of day, month and year are also significant.

Lunar position has been shown in some studies to be a contributing factor to fish and game activity, but the approach of weather systems (high-pressure systems typically preceded by low-pressure systems) is usually a more decisive factor than the moon in influencing fish to bite and animals to feed.

Along with the moon and the weather, water temperature and other seasonal factors play a role in how fish respond to bait.

One of the best ways to measure those factors is to keep a journal of conditions and of what is happening during your outings. An almanack may be helpful in making you aware of what is going on in nature, but your own experiences in specific habitats and at specific times of year may be the most useful sources of information. More effective than tables of solar and lunar position is your connection to the earth.

All that being said, "The Moon and the Weather" section of *Poor Will's Almanack for 2017* provides a list of pivotal dates for the arrival of high-pressure systems, with comments on the effect of the moon on those systems.

Lunar and frontal movements can be helpful in planning your outings since fish, game, livestock and people tend to feed more and are more active as the barometer is falling one to three days before these weather systems.

In addition, many people find that livestock, children, fish and game are more active (and dieting is more difficult) when the moon is overhead: at midday when the moon is new, in the afternoon and evening when the moon is in its first quarter, at night when the moon is full and in its third quarter, in the morning when the moon is in its fourth quarter. Second-best lunar times occur when the moon is below your location, 12 hours before or after those times noted above.

See the "Peak Activity Times for Creatures" section of each monthly section of the *Almanack* for a guide to lunar position and corresponding behavior.

About the S.A.D. Stress Index

The S.A.D. Stress Index in each monthly chapter of the *Almanack* is one way of measuring those natural phenomena which are assumed to be related to seasonal affective disorder (S.A.D.): the day's length, the probable percentage of sunlight, and the weather. In order to create the Index, each of those factors was given a value from zero to 25, and then the three values were combined onto a scale of one to 75. The higher the number, the greater the stress. Index readings are most useful in combination with a record of your own moods. Reference to the Index when you feel out of sorts may be a way of getting a feel for how seasonal affective disorder influences your life.

The Calendar of Feast Days

In this section, the *Almanack* lists the days of the year on which farmers, gardeners and homesteaders might expect the public to have increased interest in their livestock or produce. The "Calendar" is also useful when one is planning strategies for marketing to particular groups.

Almanack Phenology: When... Then

Many of the events of the annual cycle recur year after year in a regular order. A year-to-year record of this order is a record of the rates at which solar energy flows to and through living things. They are the arteries of the land. By tracing their responses to the sun, Phenology may eventually shed some light on that ultimate enigma, the land's inner workings.

Aldo Leopold, *A Phenological Record for Sauk and Dane Counties, Wisconsin, 1935-1945 (1947)*

The phenological observer who watches "what-happens-when" in the local world of nature gathers and collates pieces of information. To the backyard phenologist, all these pieces are useful and all have meaning.

The natural history of any region offers an endless number of such data or primary sources, and the process of collecting and cataloging them can contribute to a greater understanding of the "land's inner workings" and to making sense of the world.

The "Almanack Phenology: When – Then" section of *Poor Will's Almanack for 2017* offers some examples of connections between certain events in nature. These and so many other connections wait to be observed and contemplated by the almanack reader.

A Note About Almanack Literature

Thirty-three years ago in February, my first *Poor Will's Almanack* appeared as a column in *The Yellow Springs News* in Yellow Springs, Ohio. A third of a century of putting together almanacks has given me a chance to explore everything from prostitution in my home town to personal existential angst.

If my columns have helped me clarify what I thought a small town should be, it also helped me clarify what I should be.

Watching the seasons became a process of self-definition as well as definition of habitat. Through the years, I continue to find new ways to see the commonplace and to define home.

Toward the end of the 1980s, I began to ask for reader stories, and "Almanack Literature" was born. People wrote all kinds of things for my column: memory stories, outhouse tales, narratives about unusual occurrences and special animals. That these narratives are juxtaposed with a nature journal and astronomical notes may seem somewhat strange to some. And before I started writing almanacks, I would never have foreseen the combinations, for example, of an outhouse story with my very personal ruminations.

The almanack, however, is a supremely eclectic genre; if an introvert with a lonely sense of fun were to select a way to combine both parts of his or her personality, almanacking might just be the path to follow.

So *Poor Will* has not only helped me to take myself less seriously, but has also infused a community and sense of humor into my solitary reflections and compilations. The inclusion of stories by my contributors is organic to the process. We are all in this together.

Using Calendars of Blooming Plants

A floating chronology is a sequence of events whose dates are all known in relation to one another, yet the time when the sequence as a whole occurred is unknown.

Martin Gorst, *Measuring Eternity*

Most of the notations about natural history in *Poor Will's Almanack* are based on my observations over more than 30 years at average elevations along the 40th Parallel. The flowering dates in this calendar are approximate, suggesting sequence and context. Although dates on most flower calendars are site-specific, this Almanack's "floating calendar" can be used in many areas of the country by adjusting the sequence described here to fit local conditions.

INDEX OF ALMANACK LITERATURE
Stories by Readers
Of *Poor Will's Almanack*

Find these stories by going to the **end** of the section that begins with the following dates.

INDEX OF ESSAYS
by Bill Felker
and Location in the *Almanack*

Find these essays by going to the **first page** of each monthly section.

Bill Felker

Part II
An Overview of the Forty-Eight Seasons of the Year

The following seasonal notes offer a nature-based outline of the year in which what happens to plants and animals can be used to tell time.

All seasons are constructs of individual events and objects. Without those parts, there is no whole. Seasons are also like moveable feasts that change according to latitude and altitude.

For example, although early spring comes at different times of the year in different locations, that season usually displays many markers or events that are similar from place to place. The daffodils bloom in Georgia earlier than in Wisconsin; however, daffodils are markers of early spring in both locations.

The observer in Maine or New Orleans will see some similar events in nature at different times. In many cases, a person may see a dramatic compression of the seasons, in which the landmarks of early summer blend with the landmarks of middle and late summer.

Still, seasons are always the sum of their parts, and those parts (rather than the solstices or the Gregorian calendar) define the season.

If readers not only observe what is happening with the Sun and stars, but also follow the floral and faunal constellations of the landscape around them, they will come to know where they are by what lies around them. That knowledge, imperfect as it may always be, is the source of a beginner's mind which connects the observer to the world.

Being aware of just one or two elements in each of the following seasons, you may be able to find your own season in your own place. Instead of a calendar, you will have a map of time and space.

Deep Winter

Phase 1: When Black Bears Emerge from Hibernation in the South: Deep winter is the coldest time of the year throughout the United States. In the North, precipitation falls in the form of snow; rivers and lakes and the ground freeze solid. At bird feeders, sparrows become louder and more voracious as courting time follows the lengthening days. The final leaves come down, and new growth immediately begins again. Anticipating that growth, black bears come out to feed in the semi-tropical undergrowth.

Phase 2: When Foxes Frolic: Under the

cold veneer of deep winter, the natural year quickens. Nighttime excursions of skunks, an increase in opossum activity, the frolicking mating of foxes, the prophetic calls of overwintering robins, the occasional passage of bluebirds, the mating of owls and the disappearance of autumn seeds all offer counterpoint to the subdued winter silence and chill.

Phase 3: When Asian Ladybugs Emerge: Asian ladybug emerging season calls out ladybugs onto sunny windowsills this time of the month. Housefly emerging season sometimes accompanies the appearance of the intrusive ladybeetles. Florist's daffodil, tulip, crocus and hyacinth season opens when ladybugs emerge: retail outlets introduce flowering spring bulbs, either potted or as cut flowers.

Late Winter
Phase 1: When Cardinals Sing: Winter's third phase, late winter, is the vestibule to early spring, growing the cardinal song that fills the mornings, rousing small mammals to courtship.

Migrant crows join the resident crows, often arriving with a major thaw. Juncos cluster, readying for migration north. The orange fruit of the evergreen winterberry (euonymus) vines and the bittersweet vines have completed their self-seeding. Overwintering robins eat and scatter the crab apples.

Phase 2: When Pussy Willows Start to Pop: Robins and bluebirds often arrive in the Lower Midwest when pussy willows open. Mourning doves join the cardinals in song, and the great chorus that lasts deep into summer is well underway. The first dandelions can be flowering, snow crocus and henbit budding. Sometimes moss is growing on logs, when pussy willows are popping from their hulls.

Phase 3: When Maple Sap Runs in the South: In the Ohio Valley, garlic planted in late November has pushed out of the ground, is already several inches high. The maple sap is already running in the South and will soon rise in the North. Under the sun of central Florida, dragonflies are hunting in the wetlands, and new insect broods foreshadow spring throughout the Gulf states.

Early Spring
Phase 1: When Monarch Butterflies Come North: Along the Gulf of Mexico, violet, wintersweet, winter Honeysuckle, Lenten rose, strawberry and jasmine blooming seasons begin in early spring. In northern Mexico, monarch butterfly

migration season moves the monarchs toward the Texas border. They will arrive in the United States during mid to late March, and their offspring will find the North in middle summer.

Phase 2: When Ducks Seek Nesting Sites: The benign thaws of early spring tell mallards, canvasback ducks and killdeer to check out sites for laying eggs. Milder afternoons call out moths and water striders.

Flocks of red-winged blackbirds and robins arrive in the fields. Mourning cloak butterflies appear, and chipmunks come out to play and mate in the dwindling woodpiles. Horned owlets hatch in the woods.

Phase 3: When Snowdrops and Aconites Bloom: When the earliest bulbs come into flower, woodchucks dig up the hillsides, making new dens.

Meadowlark, eagle, killdeer, horned lark, red-winged blackbird and duck migration seasons accelerate the appearance of spring as steelhead and walleye fishing seasons gradually unfold in the Great Lakes.

Phase 4: When Cherry Trees Bud in Washington, D.C.: Cherry trees bud in Washington, D.C. about the same time that coltsfoot flowers in the hills of West Virginia. In the Deep South, late daffodils accompany the peak of azalea bloom, and the peak of desert wildflower blossoms in the Southwest. Along the Platte River in Nebraska, sandhill cranes assemble for their migration north when cherry trees bud in Washington, D.C.

Phase 5: When Robins Sing in the Dark: When the robin chorus begins before sunrise, then pollen forms on pussy willow catkins, and the first mosquito bites.

When robins sing before dawn, the first tulip bud has formed. The early leaves of honeysuckle bushes green the countryside, and the tree line is tinged with red from flowering maples.

Phase 6: When the Great Wildflower Bloom Begins: The final week of early spring brings may apple and toad trillium emerging season on sunny slopes, and the first days of leafing out season for willows, mock orange and buckeyes. Forsythia blossom season starts throughout the Lower Midwest

When temperatures rise to the 60s for a few days, the Great Wildflower Bloom Time arrives with bluebells, twinleaf, bloodroot, small-flowered bittercress and hepatica budding and then bursting into bloom.

Middle Spring
Phase 1: When the Frogs Cry Out in the Night: American toad and green frog song season announces the first phase of middle spring, as well as the first week of duckling and gosling hatching season.

Field corn planting season and oats planting season get underway. Sweet corn planting season and lettuce planting season are open in the garden. And the lawn is long enough to cut.

Phase 2: When Strawberries Flower: When strawberries flower, cowslip is just opening in the wetlands. Early peach trees are in bloom, along with forsythia, pears, quince, star and pink magnolias, cherries and the last of the *cornus mas*. Branches of the multiflora roses are almost completely covered with foliage. Pale spikes of lizard's tail are long and soft.

Phase 3: The Great Dandelion and Fruit Tree Bloom: The Great Dandelion Bloom is the most common and the most radical marker for the third phase of middle spring. Of course, a few dandelions started blooming in early spring, and often they bloom year around. The *Great* Dandelion Flowering and The *Great* Fruit Tree Bloom however, begin in the Deep South, where middle spring comes much earlier than it

does in the North, and it spreads up through the Border States like robins, reaching the 40th Parallel, the lateral midline of the United States, in April and then creeps the North in May.

Late Spring
Phase 1: When Tadpoles Swim in the Shallows: Black tadpoles swim in the backwaters when late spring arrives. Bass move to the shallows. Termites swarm. Bumblebees come out with the sun. Cabbage butterflies visit the fresh cabbage sets. June bugs begin their evening flights.

Allergy season intensifies with late spring, the time when trees are in full flower throughout the Great Plains, the Northeast, the Northwest and the Rocky Mountains. And in the Southeast, all the grasses are coming into bloom.

Most dandelions have gone to seed in the Ohio Valley, and ruby-throated hummingbirds arrive at their feeders throughout the North. Nettles are waist high along the fencerows. In drier years, farmers have put in all the corn and soybeans.

Phase 2: When Daddy Longleg Spiders Appear: When you see your first daddy longlegs, oak leaves are the size of a squirrel's ear almost everywhere. Some maples are fully leafed, and some are dropping seeds. The high tree line is completely alive all across the country either with new glowing foliage or orange buds or golden flowers.

Meadows host white clover and red clover, tall meadow rue, catchweed, fire pink and angelica. Blackberries, black raspberries, multiflora roses and elderberry bushes bloom in the hedgerows. Mock orange, locusts, wild cherry trees, yellow poplars (tulip trees), Kousa dogwoods and peonies join the early iris, sweet Williams, climbing roses and rhododendrons.

In the deep woods, late Jack-in-the-pulpit, nodding trillium, Solomon's seal, columbine, waterleaf, shooting star and clustered snakeroot bloom.

Phase 3: When Azaleas Lose Their Petals: When azaleas lose their petals, daisies and the first clematis and the first cinquefoil open all the way, the first strawberry ripens, and the first swallowtail butterflies visit the star of Bethlehem and bleeding hearts. The last quince flowers fall, and lilacs decay.

The pink and violet of sweet rockets replace the purple wild phlox in the woods and pastures. All of the buttercups blossom, and the first pyrethrums forecast the poppies. Horseradish and comfrey are budding.

Phase 4: When Honeysuckles Bloom:
When honeysuckles blossom, then mulberries and wild grapes flower. Multiflora roses, spirea, yellow sweet clover, Canadian thistles, privet and yellow poplars bud. Evergreens have four to six inches of new growth.

Sycamore and ginkgo leaves are half size, and the rest of the maples are filling in. Rhododendrons follow the azaleas, joined by the raspberries and blackberries. Wild strawberries climb, bright yellow, through the purple ivy and the sticky catchweed. Blue-eyed grass is open.

Early Summer
Phase 1: When the High Foliage is Complete: When the high foliage is complete, then the wild multiflora roses and the domestic tea roses bloom, the last Osage and black walnut flowers fall, clustered snakeroot hangs with pollen in the shade, and parsnips, goatsbeard and sweet clovers take over the roadsides. Rare swamp valerian blossoms by the water, and common timothy pushes up from its sheaths in all the alleyways.

Phase 2: When Grackles Feed Their Young: Mother grackles and robins are cleaning their nests, often depositing the white droppings of their babies in birdbaths or ponds. Canadian geese are molting, now that all of their goslings have hatched.

Whiteflies attack azaleas. Eastern tent caterpillars leave their tents. Inspired by all the insects, spiders weave the first major network of cobwebs across the woodland paths.

Phase 3: When Parsnips Flower: The peak of the parsnips in the fields is the high time for the wetlands' poison hemlock and angelica. In the shade, poison ivy, fire pink and honewort are flowering. At the edge of the forest, wild plants include blue-eyed grass, silver yarrow, yellow sedum, bright moneywort, fire pink, daisies, yellow sweet clover, wild roses, wild iris, dock and smooth brome grass. In the garden, the blue veronica, yellow coreopsis, deep purple loosestrife and the first wave of the floribunda roses come into flower.

Phase 4: The Time of Wild Black Raspberries: In the time of wild black raspberries, leafhoppers and Japanese beetles are more troublesome. Chiggers and ticks are more aggressive. The first woolly bear caterpillars, harbingers of winter, cross the road. Snapping turtles and mud turtles are hatching.

Cattails are almost fully developed. May apples are ready to harvest in the woods. Blackberries have set fruit, even in the coldest years. Black walnuts are about half their full size, Osage fruits the size of golf balls. The common orange ditch lilies reach full bloom. Asiatic and Oriental lilies gather momentum, pacing the bee balm.

Middle Summer
Phase 1: When Thistles Unravel:

When thistles come undone, then all the middle-summer flowers are in bloom. Purple loosestrife, lizard's tail, Queen Anne's lace, purple coneflower, wild petunia, bouncing bet, dayflower, sow thistle, white vervain, dogbane, black-eyed Susan, leatherflower, figwort, lesser stitchwort, square-stemmed germander, pokeweed, St. John's wort, teasel, wild lettuce, wood mint, wood nettle, leafcup, touch-me-not, lopseed and avens are all blossoming in the woods and fields.

Phase 2: When Cicadas Emerge: Corn tassels and corn pollen are more plentiful when the annual cicadas sing. Goldenrod can be four feet tall. Lupine pods break apart and spread their seeds. White snakeroot, ironweed, boneset, wingstem, tall coneflowers and gray-headed coneflowers are budding as the towering yucca flowers disappear. Midseason hostas, liatris and obedient plant open. Throughout the whole country, more wildflowers blossom now than at any other time.

Phase 3: When the Tide of Summer Turns: At the start of summer ebb tide, the land is on the early side of cicada song and fireflies are still vigorous. The first katydids begin to chant after dark, and crickets intensify their calls. Woolly bear caterpillars and Japanese beetles become more common. Thistledown unravels more dramatically when summer's tide has turned. Seed pods form on trumpet creepers. Catalpa beans are fat and long.

Phase 4: When Blackberries Redden: The fkatydid voices, the slow rise of cricket song, the quieting of the early morning birds and the first restless flights of geese are clear signs of this phase of middle summer, the phase during which blackberries darken.

Black raspberries disappear, while the second crop of red raspberries ripens. Osage fruits are bigger than apples. Acorns are as big as marbles. Sumac staghorns are velvety red. Catalpa beans grow long and firm. There is a scent of August in the morning air, the smell of windfall fruit, of spent flowers and leaves.

Phase 5: When Late-Year Crickets Sing:
As cicadas and katydids and new crickets define the days and nights, the yellowing locust and buckeye leaves and the brown garlic mustard give a sense of fall to the woods. Shiny spicebush, boxwood, greenbrier and poison ivy berries have formed. Ironweed and wingstem come into bloom. Black walnuts are almost autumn size.

Late Summer
Phase 1: When Ragweed Blooms: The first week of ragweed time is the first week of late summer. In the mornings, cardinals and doves still sing briefly half an hour before dawn. Robins still give long singsong performances throughout the day. Blue jays still care for their young, whining and flitting through the bushes. Bullfrogs still call in the ponds. But by the end of the week, meadowlarks and plovers fly south, leading the first sizeable bird migrations of the year's second half.

Phase 2: When Black Walnut Trees Start to Lose Their Leaves: Cottonwoods are yellowing while acorns fall to the ground and black walnut foliage is thinning. Locust leaves turn brown, damaged by leaf miners. Violet Joe Pye weed grays like thistledown. The prickly teasel dies. Fruit of the bittersweet ripens.

Spicebush berries redden. Tall goldenrod is heading up. Rose pinks and great blue lobelia color the waysides. In the thunderstorms of late summer, green acorns fall to the sweet rocket growing back among the budding asters.

Phase 3: When Yellow Jackets Feed on the Windfalls: Fall webworms crawl from their silver webs. Bees and wasps are everywhere in the fields. Monarchs and swallowtails continue their passage through the gardens. Cricket chants dominate the nights. In orchards and yards, yellow jackets come to eat the fallen apples and peaches.

Phase 4: When Wild Plums Are Ripe for Jam: When you can find tall ironweed, wingstem, wild oxeye, small-flowered agrimony, tall bellflower, white snakeroot, wild lettuce, sundrops, heal-all, wild cucumber, jumpseed, tall coneflower, clearweed, touch-me-not and goldenrod all in bloom, then wild plums are ripe for jam, and woodland grapes are purple. Puffball mushrooms emerge among spring's rotting stems and leaves. Greenbrier berries darken.

Phase 5: When Asters Bloom: White and violet asters, orange beggarticks, bur marigolds, late field goldenrod, and zigzag goldenrod come into bloom, blending with the last of the purple ironweed, yellow sundrops and wingstem, blue chicory and lobelia, golden touch-me-nots and showy coneflowers. In gardens, knotweed is flowering, as are latest hostas, the stonecrop and virgin's bower.

Early Fall

Phase 1: When Soybean Fields Turn Brown: Now the soybean fields are rusty brown and yellow. Touch-me-nots are popping. Wood nettle seeds are black. Wingstem, clearweed and ironweed complete their cycle. Buckeyes are starting to burst from their hulls. More black walnuts, more hickory nuts, more acorns come down. The huge pink mallows of the wetlands have died, heads dark, leaves disintegrating. Scattered in the pastures, the milkweed pods are full, straining, and ready to open. Mullein stalks stand bare like withered cacti. In the perennial garden, late hostas discard their petals.

Phase 2: When Jumpseeds Jump: Touch-me-nots are still blooming in the woods, but their foliage is breaking down as the last pods burst. Asters, goldenrod and beggarticks start to go to seed, everything seeming to unravel at once.

Wingstem and ironweed are done

blossoming. The last jumpseeds are jumping from the jumpseed plant. Boneset and white snakeroot darken. Beggarticks are almost ready to stick to your clothing. Roadside sunflowers and Jerusalem artichokes enter their final weeks.

Phase 3: When Milkweed Pods Open: When the milkweed pods come open, then frost season is really on the way, and Canadian geese, great-crested flycatchers, blue-gray gnatcatchers, ruby-throated hummingbirds, eastern wood peewees and bank swallows move down their flyways toward the Gulf of Mexico.

Buzzards gather at their roosts. Crows are the only birds to call before dawn. Monarch butterflies become more numerous, still visit the late phlox and the zinnias in the afternoon sun; other insects, however, become less common in the field and garden as the number of pollen-bearing flowers dwindles. Spiders understand; they weave fewer webs.

Phase 4: Time of Second Spring: As early fall comes to a close, purple deadnettle and garlic mustard sprout. Wood mint grows new stalks. Watercress revives. Waterleaf slowly reappears along the rivers. April's sweet Cicely, May's sweet rockets, ragwort, dock, and poison hemlock, June's cinquefoil and hollyhocks, July's avens and caraway, September's zigzag goldenrod and small-flowered asters all send up fresh leaves. Moss thickens on rotting logs.

Middle Fall

Phase 1: When Monarch Butterflies Depart: The last monarchs depart for Mexico as the high canopy thins and the burning bush turns scarlet. The ashes, redbuds and hickories shed quickly, and the land enters full maple-turn and middle fall. Many catalpas are down, beans left swinging in the wind. Ginkgo fruits, which will be on the ground by late November, are turning pink. Box elders, poplars, elms, red mulberries and sycamores are mottled.

Phase 2: When Maples Reach Full Color: The chemical changes in the foliage that became noticeable six weeks ago accelerate until the fragile landscape turns all at once. Shagbark hickories, maples, sweet gums, oaks, sassafras and sycamores reach peak color. Blueberry bushes are completely red. In the cooler, wetter nights, crickets and katydids are weakening. Only a few swallowtails and fritillaries visit the garden, and just a few fireflies glow in the grass. Out in the fields, almost all the wildflowers have gone to seed. Wild cucumber fruits are dry and empty. Hosta pods are splitting. Wild asparagus yellows by the roadsides.

Phase 3: Katydids Fall Silent: In the last week of middle fall, the katydids become quiet, and the oaks and the Osage, white mulberries, magnolias, ginkgoes and the late black and sugar maples move towards full color. The second tier of leaves, consisting mostly of the early maples, is coming down. (In the first tier were the ashes and box elders, locusts and buckeyes.)

As foliage thins, eastern phoebes, catbirds, turkey vultures and house wrens depart. Vast flocks of robins are fluttering, chattering, whinnying, and moving south through the high trees along the river valleys.

Late Fall
Phase 1: When Goldenrod Is Tufted Like Cotton: Sometimes the maple and white mulberry leaves that survived to this point drop in a day. The ginkgoes do the same; they can shatter overnight into a shining circle below their limbs. Willows, though, are only half turned. Decorative pear trees are still green, prolonging an illusion of September. Silver maples seem to be untouched by the radical shift in the

season; they hold until the nights go into the teens.   Dogwoods will be pink, magnolias gold, oaks red-orange for a few days longer.   Beneath them, privet and spicebush will remain strong for another two weeks.

Phase 2: When Witch Hazels Bloom: Along the highways, ironweed seeds are soft and white when witch hazels bloom. Goldenrod and thimbleweed are tufted like cotton, their foliage deep chocolate brown. Most of the milkweed pods have opened. A few blackberry bushes are bare; others are still red and purple.   Mums are past their best, and pokeweed berries shrivel and fall.

Phase 3: When Skunk Cabbage First Emerges: When skunk cabbage appears, new winter wheat has turned fields bright green again.   Lawns grow back; they can be long and thick beneath the fallen leaves.   Garlic mustard that sprouted fourteen months ago has persevered with only a cluster of basal leaves all summer and fall; the worst cold will not kill it. Beside the hesitant spears of skunk cabbage, colors deepen. Protected by the streams, watercress shines; dock and ragwort come back beside the dead field grasses.

Phase 4: When Sandhill Cranes Depart:
All but a few shriveled staghorns have
fallen from the sumac when the sandhill
cranes leave their last feeding grounds in
the North. Thistles are bedraggled, foliage
curled and shriveled. Fields of dry
goldenrod heads glow in the sun, more
exotic than when they were in flower. Box
elder seeds shimmer in the frost. Sharp
burdock burrs are poised, waiting for you
to brush against them.

Early Winter

Phase 1: When Pear Leaves Fall: When
sunset reaches its earliest time of the
year, the brittle leaves of the pear trees
fall. This is the time during which the
second bloom of forsythia ends, when
witch hazel blossoms wither, and the last
of the golden beeches, the willows, Osage
and oaks come down.

The corn and soybean harvests are
usually complete all around the county,
and development of winter wheat slows in
the cold. New garlic shoots are firm and
green, but they have stopped growing and
remain at their middle-autumn height.
The Christmas tree harvest has begun,
and the last poinsettias have come north.

Phase 2: When the Last Gulls Migrate:
When the last gulls migrate, then the
northern states are locked in winter cold.

Throughout greenhouses and under grow lights, however, nursery workers and gardeners plant and care for the seeds of tender plants that will be set out when the danger of frost is past.

Phase 3: When Pruning Time Begins: When winter moves all the way down from Canada, then lakes and rivers start to freeze. Under the auspices of the cold, the season of winter pruning commences. It is time to force more bulbs so that they bloom in deep winter, to seed more bedding plants, to nurse annuals brought in from the cold.

Phase 4: When Spring Starts North Again: In central Florida, red maples open, and Jessamine produces its yellow blossoms. No matter the dramatic differences between the last phase of early winter in the North and South, this time is the gateway to the coldest time of year as well as the door to spring.

Part III
The Months of the Year

Bill Felker

JANUARY 2017

*Therefore all seasons
shall be sweet to thee,
whether the summer clothe
the general earth with greenness,
or the redbreast sit and sing
betwixt the tufts of snow on the bare branch
of mossy apple tree, while the nigh thatch
smokes in the sun-thaw;
whether the eve-drops fall
heard only in the trances of the blast;
or if the secret ministry of frost
shall hang them up in silent icicles,
quietly shining in the quiet moon.*

Samuel Taylor Coleridge

The Gregorian Calendar for January

S	M	T	W	T	F	S
1	2	3	4	5	6	7
8	9	10	11	12	13	14
15	16	17	18	19	20	21
22	23	24	25	26	27	28
29	30	31				

Spring Meaning

The essayist Rebecca Solnit writes that "the very notion of giving meaning to something is premised on a cosmology in which things don't have it yet."

So, for example, when I talk about the meaning of spring, I am entering a verbal landscape in which the different elements of that season make no necessary sense in and by themselves.

Spring and the meaning of spring are not self-evident, are not a priori notions. They depend on my experience and construction of them, after the fact, a posteriori. They balance on synthesis and projection, on acceptance and on letting go.

In January, my encounter with the reclusive spring is still a fabrication of faith, of hope, recollection, longing. When sometimes my imagination fails, it seems that winter will last forever, that my dreams of warmth will never come true.

But Rebecca Solnit's statement – that giving meaning is premised on a cosmology in which things don't yet have meaning – uncovers the benign and beckoning passivity of the land around me.

I remind myself that even though the world appears so vast, even though it seems so cold and bare now, it is the I, it is the mind, the self alone, that is able to perceive and uncover Earth's meaning and to make the spring come true.

The Tufted Titmouse Moon and the Lenten Rose Moon

One of the first songbirds to forecast the end of winter is the tufted titmouse, its clear repetitive songs cutting through the cold wind and overcast skies. As other birds join the morning chorus, Lenten roses (hellebores) come into bloom behind them. Among the earliest flowers to bloom, the Lenten rose opens as aconites and snowdrops blossom in protected areas. Maple sap runs when hellebores bloom in February, and most of the nation's lambs and kids are born.

January 5: The Tufted Titmouse Moon enters its second quarter at 2:47 p.m.

January 10: Lunar perigee (when the moon is closest to Earth)

January 12: The moon is full at 6:34 a.m.

January 19: The moon enters its final quarter at 5:13 p.m.

January 22: Lunar apogee (when the moon is farthest from Earth)

January 27: The Lenten Rose Moon is new at 7:07 p.m.

The S.A.D. Index

January brings the year's coldest weather to every state of the Union, and seasonal affective disorder is more frequent than at any time during the winter. On the other hand, by the time the moon is new (January 27), progress has been made in the day's length as well as in the quality of the weather, keeping the S.A.D Index from reaching into the middle 70s.

Key for Interpreting the S.A.D. Index:
Totals of 75 to 65: Severe Stress
64 to 50: Severe to moderate stress
49 to 35: Moderate stress
34 to 25: Light to moderate stress
24 and below: Light stress

Day	Clouds	Weather	Daylight	Totals
January 1:	25	24	25	74
January 15:	25	25	24	74
January 30:	25	22	22	69

The Sun

Perihelion, the point at which the Earth and the Sun are closest to one another in 2017, occurs on January 4 at 9:00 a.m. The Sun enters the late winter constellation of Aquarius on the 21st of January.

The Planets

♃ ♄ ♂ ♀

Venus is the evening star, low in the southwest after dark, close to Mars. Giant Jupiter rises out of the east in Virgo after midnight, taking its place as the morning star. Saturn follows Libra in Ophiuchus before dawn.

The Stars

Shifting to the center of the sky these evenings in deep winter, Orion is the night clock of winter, his hands telling high noon of the season at midnight as January and the cold deepen. By spring equinox, he will have slipped into the far west in the evening. Rising near dawn, his

Dog Star, Sirius, prophesies the Dog Days of July.

The Shooting Stars

January's shooting stars are the Quadrantids; they appear early in the first week of the month at the rate of about 35 per hour. Look for them after midnight in the eastern sky near Arcturus.

Calendar of Feast Days and Holidays for Farmers, Gardeners and Homesteaders

January 13, 2017: Mardi Gras season begins around this time, lasting until the big celebration on February 28.

January 28, 2017: Tet, Vietnamese New Year and Chinese New Year (The Year of the Rooster): The Chinese market is often strong throughout the winter, favoring lambs and kids (but not roosters) in the 70-pound live-weight range.

Farming and Gardening with the Moon

Under lights, sow flats of bedding plants as the moon waxes. Flowers such as salvia, coleus, geraniums and petunias can be started now. Seed cold-weather broccoli, kale, collards, cabbage and celery for setting out in early spring. Also plant the spring garden throughout the Deep South as the moon is waxing. Frost-seed pastures throughout the Border States at the same time.

The best lunar times to work with your livestock during January will be around the time the moon enters its second phase and its fourth phase. According to a number of studies, the moon exerts less influence on ocean tides and on human and animal behavior during these periods between new and full moon.

After full moon, plant bulbs, shrubs and trees throughout the southern half of the United States. Do your pruning everywhere: take out suckers, dead and crossing branches as the moon wanes. Don't prune what will bloom before June, and wait for July or August for the maples. Expect sap to run in the maples throughout the South as the traditional

January thaw moves across the nation and the moon waxes.

In the North, purchase grass seed for frost-seeding the lawn; get clover ready for frost-seeding the pasture; be ready to put in spring oats and barley, too. Increase energy feeds to animals in unusually severe weather. Many people believe that feeding energy foods in the evening produces the best results.

The Moon and the Weather

Weather history indicates that cold waves will cross the Mississippi around the dates listed below. The fronts pass through the West 24 to 48 hours prior to their arrival in the Midwest; they reach the East 24 to 48 hours later.

Major storms are most likely to occur during the following periods: January 1 – 3, 8 – 12, 19 – 24. Lunar perigee on the 10th, full moon on 12th and new moon on the 27th are likely to increase the possibility of severe weather.

January 1

Cold and blowing snow usually attack the North on New Year's Day. In the Deep South, rain and highs only in the 40s are the rule. A secondary disturbance often causes additional problems on the 2nd and 3rd.

January 5

Thunder and maybe even a tornado can be expected in the South as this second January front moves across the nation's gardens and pastures. In the North, the temperatures usually get considerably colder after the passage of this high. A low-pressure system that precedes the next weather system, the January 10th front, is often associated with the first major winter storm of the new year.

January 10

The middle of January's second week is one of the worst storm periods of the year. Blizzards are likely to occur at this time, and below-zero morning lows may freeze the water in your troughs, along with the pipes in your crawl space and in the barn. Lunar perigee on the 10th and full moon on the 12th will strengthen the January 10th system.

January 15

Along with this front come the coldest two weeks of the year (on average)

for animals and people. Across the
northern tier of states, days on which the
temperature does not rise above zero
toccur more often than at any time of year.

January 20

During the "January Thaw" period,
which usually occurs between this front
and the January 25th front, odds rise
again for blizzards in the North and hard
rains in the South. The moon will be
entering its weak final quarter on the
19th, and it will be at apogee on the 22nd,
favoring a dramatic warm-up across the
Great Plains and the East.

January 25

Secondary frontal conditions,
sometimes carrying moist Gulf air, can set
off powerful blizzards around the 27th.
And the moon will be turning new on the
27th, increasing the chances for heavy
precipitation, followed by more cold.

January 31

This weather system is almost
always followed by the Groundhog Day
Thaw. But don't be tricked. The first bad
front of February will bring temperatures
back to their mid-January depths.

Almanack Phenology: When...Then

When the first crocus leaves push up in milder years, then the first pussy willow catkin could be open just a crack.

When sparrows chatter near dawn, then foxes and coyotes look for mates.

When pine trees pollinate, then owls nest in the woodlots.

When daffodil foliage is an inch tall beneath the snow in Chicago, then Algerian iris will soon be blossoming in Virginia.

When white-tailed bucks start to lose their antlers in the North, then yellow Jessamine is blooming along the Gulf Coast, camellias are at their best, and avocados and papayas are ripening.

When pale Asian ladybugs emerge in the warmth of sunny windowsills, then spring flower displays appear in nurseries.

When crows migrate, then you know the sun has moved into Aquarius and the January thaw is right around the corner.

When the first fly gets in your door, then look for opossums to be wandering the backroads at night.

When cardinals sing before dawn, late winter has begun.

When you see the first flock of robins arrive from the South, you know that bluebirds have arrived, too.

Peak Activity Times for Creatures

The following guide to lunar position shows when the moon is above (Best times) or below (Second-best times) the country, and, therefore, the period during which livestock, people, fish and game are typically the most active and the hungriest.

Date	Best	Second-Best
January 1 – 4:	Afternoons	Midnight to Dawn
January 5 – 11:	Evenings	Mornings
January 12 – 18:	Midnight to Dawn	Afternoons
January 19 – 26:	Mornings	Evenings
January 27 – 31:	Afternoons	Midnight to Dawn

Almanack Literature
A Gentle Farmer
by Lou Beard, Shelby, Ohio

I was raised outside of a small, quaint town in Ohio by the name of Sycamore. It was a peaceful town where the Sycamore trees grew wild by the small creeks. My father was a loud-spoken, large-frame strong farmer, but a gentle one. He did not appear that way, nor did I think of him in that way when I was young. But now, I, as an adult older than he was when he died, realize how gentle and compassionate he was.

When the sows on the farm were ready to have their babies, he would sleep in the barn with them. He put them in individual pens by themselves, and he would sleep outside on a cot, waiting for the right time. The "cot" was a bed made from bags of hog feed stacked up and a bale of straw. When the time came, he was right there to help deliver the little ones.

As they appeared, he would clean them, wrap them in a clean, dry feed sack and lay them aside until all the babies were born, sometimes twelve or so. If one appeared weak, it would be taken to the house for extra care. He knew that if it were left behind in its weakened condition, it would not survive.

After he analyzed all the little ones, he would put them back in the care of their mother, checking on them often. I can remember two sows delivering at the same time, and Dad jumping over the divider between the sows to help both mothers deliver their babies. Most of the mother sows would deliver within a few weeks of each other, so he stayed out in the barn for weeks until it was all over.

He knew that every animal was important to his livelihood and to the welfare of the family. He did the same thing with the cows and sheep. By the time the birthing season was over in the spring, we had a bunch of healthy animals in the barn and a few, sometimes more than a few, frisky rambunctious healthy pets in the basement room we called the furnace room because it was so warm. My sister and I raised the weak babies on bottles. She warmed the milk and fed them in the middle of the night and in the mornings before school.

I can't remember ever losing a little pig or lamb. Every year it was the same thing. We got so accustomed to having little ones in the basement that it seemed strange to have an empty furnace room. I can remember crying when Dad would say, "It's time for them there babies to go out and face the real world." That was the day Mother was more than happy, but for us, it was a sad day.

FEBRUARY
2017

Now learn the signs
Of cold and heat to come,
Of drought and rain,
The secrets of the moon,
And what each wind will bring.

Virgil

The Gregorian Calendar
for February

S	M	T	W	T	F	S
			1	2	3	4
5	6	7	8	9	10	11
12	13	14	15	16	17	18
19	20	21	22	23	24	25
26	27	28				

Notes on the Community
of Fishes in Winter

When I was younger, I enjoyed fishing and the excitement of connection and of domination that accompanied it. I killed the fish I caught out of curiosity, and sometimes my mother would fry them for me. As an adult, when I killed and prepared and ate fish, I felt self-sufficient.

Now that I am old, I have a pond and four large koi. The fish have names: Buh buh (orange and white) and Bud (black and white), Princess (silver and black) and Golden Shark (gold and black). Last summer, they produced almost two-dozen fingerlings, kaleidoscopic in color.

Over the years, I have fallen in love with their ways: their caution and their eagerness, their loose hierarchies and their mutual support, their gentleness and their occasional spurts of excitement.

When the water warms above sixty degrees, they are active and swim freely. They come toward the edge of the pond when I approach with their food. The larger fish seem only mildly competitive, allowing the young to eat first if they choose.

In the winter, the cold seems to slow them all into contemplation. They move close to one another below the remnants of the lily pads. When I approach, they remain quiet, usually side-by-side, sometimes tucked together as though they were keeping each other warm. The fingerlings have a separate spot beside the lily roots, clustered like the adults in cenobitic security.

In this artificial sea, aerated by a pump and waterfall, climate controlled by a pond heater, the inhabitants lie out of danger, waiting for spring. Caring for them, I turn away from the violence of my own youth and of my species. I pretend that all is well. I make believe that the peaceful community of winter fishes is the real world and that some benevolent caretaker watches over us all.

The Lenten Rose Moon and the Robin Chorus Moon

The Lenten Rose Moon forecasts the Christian season of Lent as well as the approach of early spring. Then, roused by the Sun's rise along the ecliptic under the Robin Chorus Moon, robins begin to chant the rapidly ebbing tide of winter.

February 3: The moon enters its second phase at 11:19 p.m.
February 6: Lunar perigee (when the moon is closest to Earth)
February 10: The Lenten Rose Moon is full at 7:33 p.m.
February 18: The moon enters its final quarter at 2:33 p.m. Lunar apogee (when the moon is farthest from Earth) also

occurs on this day.
February 26: The Robin Chorus Moon is new at 9:58 a.m.

A penumbral eclipse of the full Moon will be visible as the moon rises on February 10, from approximately 5:30 p.m. to 10:00 p.m.

The S.A.D. Stress Index

The likelihood of seasonal stress begins to fall in February. The average amount of sunlight increases, especially in the South, the night is shrinking, temperatures rise, and the arrival of early spring offers the promise of relief from seasonal affective disorders.

Key for Interpreting the S.A.D. Index:
Totals of 75 to 65: S.A.D. Severe Stress
64 to 50: Severe to moderate stress
49 to 35: Moderate stress
34 to 25: Light to moderate stress
24 and below: Low stress

Day	Clouds	Weather	Daylight	Totals
February 1:	24	20	22	64
February 10:	23	23	19	65
February 20:	22	19	18	59
February 28:	22	19	17	58

The Sun

On the 18th of February, the Sun reaches halfway to equinox. This landmark in the solar year is called Cross-Quarter Day. On February 20, the Sun enters the Early Spring constellation of Pisces.

The Planets

♃ ♄ ♂ ♀

Venus moves retrograde into Pisces this month, remaining the evening star, still accompanied by Mars. Jupiter – residing in Virgo through October – rises after dark and travels across the sky through the night, competing with Arcturus of Bootes for prominence. Remember that Arcturus will twinkle, while Jupiter's light remains steady. Saturn rides the heavens in Ophiuchus, appearing several hours before dawn.

The Stars

When you get up before dawn, look due south above the distant tree line. The square-like formation you see will be Libra. Above it, the stars of Serpens lead toward the Corona Borealis, a formation that looks like a bright stellar necklace. In the far west, Regulus is the brightest star. In the east, the brightest one is Vega.

Calendar of Feast Days and Holidays for Farmers, Gardeners and Homesteaders

February 19, 2017: Meatfare Sunday, the last Sunday to eat meat before Orthodox Christian Easter

February 27, 2017: Dominican Republic Independence Day: Areas that have a sizeable population of residents from the Dominican Republic may show an increase in sales of lambs and kids that weigh between 20 to 35 pounds.

February 28, 2017: Mardi Gras: This is the last great feast before Lent begins.

Farming and Gardening with the Moon

Lunar conditions are favorable for the seeding of bedding plants and the taking of cuttings from mother plants after new moon (near the beginning and the end of this month). Frost-seed pastures and seed the lawn along and below the 40th Parallel.

Also under the dark moon, treat ash, bittersweet, fir, elm, flowering fruit trees, hawthorn, juniper, lilac, linden, maple, oak, pine, poplar, spruce, sweet gum, tulip tree and willow for scales and mites.

Spray trees with dormant oil when temperatures rise into the upper 30s or 40s. The best chances of experiencing those temperatures in northern states will occur between February 15 and 23. Expect maple sap flow to slow down after Snowdrop Winter, which typically occurs between the 24th and the 27th.

Between new and full moon, seed vegetables that produce their fruit above the ground. In California, plant oats and spring barley. In Texas, plant corn. Sow alfalfa and then cut hay in Arizona.

Also during these weeks, plant oats

and barley as conditions permit in the South. Spread lime, phosphate and potash as needed. In the Border States, tap trees for sap as full moon approaches.

Then after full moon, take care of livestock: trim hooves, slaughter, worm and treat for external parasites. Put in your root crops, too.

Around the yard, bulb season opens this month as far north as Chicago, with the first aconites and snowdrops opening in sheltered microclimates. It's not too early to feed your bulbs with liquid fertilizer before major blooming time begins.

The period between full moon and the moon's fourth quarter can encourage birthing, so be ready for your animals to birth up to a week early near that time of the month.

As soon as you can work the soil, plant a few peas, onions, radishes, rutabagas, asparagus crowns, spinach, turnips and carrots on milder afternoons under the dark moon in late February.

In the Southwest, put in the last of the potato crop. Then take cuttings to propagate shrubs, trees and houseplants; experiment with forsythia, pussy willow, hydrangea and spirea.

Make the first rhubarb pie in the Deep South. In the lower Midwest, the knuckles of this year's crop could be pushing out of the ground.

Frost-seeding of dormant, northern pastures and lawns may be started after the snow has receded. The February 20th cold front marks the end of the snowiest part of the year in most states.

The Moon and the Weather

Weather history indicates that cold waves will cross the Mississippi around the dates listed below. Major storms are most likely to occur on February 3, 6 -10, 14 - 18, 24 - 26. Lunar perigee on the 6th, full moon on the 10th and new moon on the 26th increase the probability of bad weather.

February 3

Precipitation is to be expected before the arrival of this front, and February 3rd is one of the February days most likely to bring dangerous storms to the Plains and tornadoes to the South. After the high-pressure system passes through, expect bitter cold to complicate birthing as well as herd and flock maintenance.

February 6
Conditions often get more challenging with the second of February's major cold fronts. Lunar perigee (when the moon is closest to Earth) on February 6th will deepen the chances for the cold.

February 11
Clouds and precipitation precede this front, and seasonal affective disorders become more intense in humans (and sometimes animals). Full moon on the 10th is expected to make conditions even more turbulent than they normally are at this time of year.

February 15
This date marks the beginning of the end of winter below the 35th Parallel. Even along the Canadian border, the frequency of highs in the teens or below starts to drop. Since mild winds from the Gulf of Mexico are likely to clash with Arctic air on the approach of this front, there is an increased likelihood of serious storms in the central states. On the other hand, apogee on the 18th could lessen the chances for tornadoes.

February 20
This front is usually fairly weak, and when the barometer drops before the next

front, it gives the fourth week of February some of the mildest days since early December. The moon this week improves the chances for gentle temperatures.

February 24

This second-last cold wave of the month brings *Snowdrop Winter* to many states. It typically signals an end to the mid-February thaw and often clashes strongly with the moist air of early spring. New moon on the 26th could keep temperatures cooler than average this year.

February 27

Although early March can bring a return of fierce cold and storms, the last weather system of February is typically mild, cutting off the hard cold of the previous system. Watch for clearing skies, too, a promise of milder conditions to come.

***

Almanack Phenology: When...Then

When you hear mourning doves singing before dawn, then organize all your buckets for tapping maple syrup.

When you hear the titmouse making its early mating calls, then test cattle for anaplasmosis and fertilize the bedding plant sprouts.

When red-winged blackbirds sing along the 40th Parallel, then the maple sap should already be running.

When the temperature reaches 55 degrees, then open up your beehives and check to see that the bees are alive and well. If you find eggs in the cells, you know the queen has not died.

When the first snowdrops emerge from their foliage (but are still not open, then be sure your cabbages, kale, Brussels sprouts and collards are sprouting under lights.

When aconites bloom, then spread fertilizer in the field and garden so that it can work its way into the ground before planting.

When maple sap runs, then prune house plants to encourage spring growth.

When the Groundhog Day Thaw arrives, then go to the wetlands to find skunk cabbage in bloom.

When the first daffodil foliage is two inches tall in Midwestern gardens, then monarch butterflies begin to migrate north from Mexico.

When you see sparrows courting, then cut branches of forsythia and pussy willows for forcing indoors.

When trees bloom early but the flowers are killed in the cold, then feed your bees to take up the slack.

When pussy willows begin to emerge,

then it is time to spray fruit trees with dormant oil.

When the first knuckles of rhubarb emerge from the ground, then it's time to plant onion sets and seed cold frames with spinach, radishes and lettuce.

When you smell skunks at night, then plant impatiens and coleus under lights for May and June.

When the red tips of peonies push out just a little from the ground, then listen for blue jays courting and watch for wild turkeys to be gathering in flocks.

When strawberry plants have new foliage, then the steelhead salmon run, which started in the fall, finally comes to a close in Lake Erie.

When wild multiflora roses sprout their first leaves in the Ohio Valley, then wildflower season has begun in the Southwest and bald eagles are laying their eggs in Yellowstone.

When tulip foliage emerges from the ground in the Lower Midwest, then horned owlets hatch in Ohio woods and sweet corn sprouts along the Gulf coast. Redbuds and azaleas bloom in Georgia, rhododendrons just starting to come in. Throughout the lowlands of Mississippi, swamp buttercups are open.

When you see the first chipmunks, then look for your mare to start cycling.

When small brown moths appear on

warmer afternoons, then ducks are looking for nesting sites. Ambystoma salamanders mate at night in the slime.

A Floating Calendar of Bloom for Wildflowers, Weeds, Garden Perennials, Shrubs and Trees

February 15: Skunk Cabbage (symplocarpus foetidus)
February 20: Snowdrop (galanthus nivalis)
　　　　　　　　Aconite (eranthis)
February 22: Snow Crocus (Crocus chrysanthus)
February 23: Iris Reticulata
February 25: Silver Maple (acer saccharinum)

Peak Activity Times for Creatures

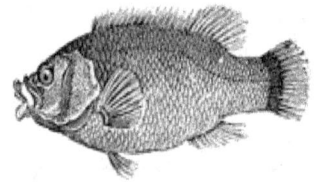

The following guide to lunar position shows when the moon is above (Best times) or below (Second-best times) the country, and, therefore, the period during which livestock, people, fish and game are typically the most active and the hungriest.

Date	Best	Second Best
February 1 – 3:	Afternoons	Midnight to Dawn
February 4 – 9:	Evenings	Mornings
February 10 – 17:	Midnight to Dawn	Afternoons
February 18 – 25:	Mornings	Evenings
February 26 – 28:	Afternoons	Midnight to Dawn

Almanack Literature
The Way It Happened: A Love Story
by Don Hoge, Burbank, Ohio

This love story started in 1942. I was in the 10th grade, and I was in study hall. The classes changed, and when I got up, I noticed this beautiful gal with perfect teeth, long hair with a headband, and a plaid jumper dress on. I didn't talk to her, and that was it. No more contact.

Now we move on to 1948. I was back from the service and was farming. So this one Saturday night, me and my buddy went to a dance at the Odd Fellows Hall in Lodi. We walked around and looked the situation over, and I couldn't believe it. There was the same girl that I had seen in 1942.

I went up and talked to her, and found out her aunt and uncle lived in Lodi, and she was a junior in college. So we danced the night away, and she could really dance.

She went out to Indiana the next

week to see relations, and told them that she had met the guy she was going to marry. But she didn't tell me.

To get on with the story, we did get married in 1949. We've been married 55 years with three kids who are all school teachers, and Mrs. Hoge retired with 28 years teaching.

So now after all these years, we are still talking, playing cards, and when you get older, everybody travels, but we have both had our health problems, she with heart trouble and me with cancer, and she can't see and I can't hear, so between the two of us we make one person.

When other people to Florida when they get old, we go south to Wooster and Polk or Ashland, Medina, Spencer and Lodi. So we are quite busy doing all of this stuff, and I am still farming, and she still has those beautiful teeth, and we are happy.

MARCH
2017

*Up from the sea
the wild north wind is blowing
Under the sky's gray arch;
Smiling, I watch the shaken elm-boughs,
knowing it is the wind of March.*

John Greenleaf Whittier

The Gregorian Calendar for March

S	M	T	W	T	F	S
			1	2	3	4
5	6	7	8	9	10	11
12	13	14	15	16	17	18
19	20	21	22	23	24	25
26	27	28	29	30	31	

Robin Chorus Synechdoche

In a grand synecdoche (in which a part stands for the whole), each event in nature always points to other events, one part linked to so many other parts, and ultimately to the whole. So the robin chorus, which begins this month along the

40th Parallel, is a mine from which one might draw out numberless concurrent happenings, all of them together making spring.

In the month of the Robin Chorus Moon when robins start their singsong calls in morning twilight, then pollen forms on pussy willow catkins, and the first mosquito bites. Moths appear at your porch light. The foliage of spiderwort, yarrow, stonecrop, mallow, phlox, columbine, coneflower, waterleaf, snow-on-the-mountain, goldenrod, buttercup, New England aster, Shasta daisy and Queen Anne's lace is coming up.

Worms rise through the ground to mate as the sun warms the mulch above them and the moon waxes. The tufted titmouse courts in spirals. Flickers and purple martins migrate, and willow trees glow yellow green. Mock orange leafs out, pacing the new privet foliage, the lilac, black raspberry, honeysuckle, multiflora rose, clematis and coralberry foliage.

Under the full Robin Chorus Moon, the first violet lungwort flowers open and bleeding hearts get bushy. The first tulip and daffodil buds form and sometimes bloom. The tree line is tinged with orange from flowering maples. Red-winged blackbirds whistle and warble in the swamps, and paired geese trumpet and converse. Turkeys gobble in the woods.

And in the last days of the final lunar phase, trillium, hepatica, Dutchman's britches, bloodroot, spring beauty, twinleaf, violet cress, and lesser celandine prophesy the sweetest time of year.

The Robin Chorus Moon follows all these and so many more events, shadows and foreshadows them, possibly causes some of them, connects them from the sky. It accompanies and enhances the tidal waves of high and low pressure that cross the land, reflects the equinoctial sun, and finally grows dark as sandhill cranes start to migrate, stirred by the more radical warming and leafing and blossoming forces of middle spring.

The Robin Chorus Moon and the Apple Blossom Moon

When the maple trees flower, then the best of sap tapping time is over, and early spring is blending to middle spring. The robin chorus fills the early mornings.

The first wave of wildflowers arrives beneath the maple blossoms Red peony stalks, barely visible a few weeks ago, have pushed above the mulch. Snowdrops, aconites and snow crocuses reach the peak of their seasons, then cede to squills and daffodils.

March 3: Lunar perigee (when the moon is closest to Earth)

March 5: The moon enters its second quarter at 6:32 a.m.

March 12: The Robin Chorus Moon is full at 9:54 a.m.

March 18: Lunar apogee (when the moon is farthest from Earth)

March 20: The moon enters its fourth quarter at 10:58 a.m.

March 27: The Apple Blossom Moon is new at 9:57 p.m.

March 30: Lunar perigee (when the moon is closest to Earth)

The S.A.D. Stress Index

Cloud cover and inclement weather continue to keep Index readings relatively high during March. The day keeps lengthening, however, and improved meteorological conditions toward the end of the month push the numbers down into the 40s after equinox.

Key for Interpreting the S.A.D. Index:

Totals of 75 to 65: Severe stress
64 to 50: Severe to moderate stress
49 to 35: Moderate stress
34 to 25: Light to moderate stress
24 and below: Low stress

Day	Clouds	Weather	Daylight	Totals
March 1:	21	18	17	56
March 10:	20	16	15	51
March 25:	18	13	12	43
March 31:	17	12	10	39

The Sun

Even though the day lengthens at different rates at different locations, equinox is still equinox at exactly 5:29 a.m. March 20 in the whole country. The Sun enters the middle spring sign of Aries on March 21.

Daylight Saving Time begins at 2:00 a.m. on Sunday, March 12.

The Planets

♃ ♄ ♂ ♀

Venus disappears as the evening star, but it reappears toward the end of the month as the morning star. Jupiter, in Virgo, has moved into the western sky before sunrise. Saturn shifts retrograde into Sagittarius, low in the southeast before dawn. Mars, passing retrograde into Aries, precedes Orion into the west before midnight.

The Stars

On March evenings, Cancer and Gemini lie in the center of the sky. Winter's Pleiades lead Orion just below the ecliptic into the northwest. Arcturus, the anchor of Bootes, comes up from the east, followed by May's Corona Borealis and milder weather. Corvus, the corn and soybean planting constellation, appears in the southeast, followed by summer's Spica.

Farming and Gardening with the Moon

Southern and Border State gardeners can seed tobacco and set out pansies, cabbages, kale, peas, collards and Brussels sprouts as the moon waxes.

It's a great time for lettuce and spinach, too, all across the southern half of the nation.

In the far North, frost-seed the pastures where the ground is still freezing and thawing on a regular basis. If you have fruit trees, complete your spraying with dormant oil before temperatures get any warmer and buds break dormancy. Mites, scale, and aphid eggs will mature quickly when the temperatures climb above 60 degrees. The insects will be more easily controlled by dormant oil spray the closer they are to hatching. Spray when the temperature is expected to stay above 40 degrees for 24 hours.

In western states and the lower Midwest, the waxing moon encourages seeds of spring oats and barley to start falling into the furrows, as long as the farmer is there to help.

As the moon wanes, livestock owners begin their regular worming of livestock in warmer parts of the country in order to reduce parasite egg counts.

And the waning moon of March is ideal for starting all root crops directly in the garden or in flats, if the weather is cold.

The Moon and the Weather

Weather history suggests that cold waves will cross the Mississippi around the dates listed below. The fronts pass through the West 24 to 48 hours prior to their arrival in the Midwest; they reach the East 24 to 48 hours later.

Major storms are most likely to occur on the days between March 9 and 14, between March 19 and 30. Lunar perigee on the 3rd and 30th, full moon on the 12th and new moon on the 27th increase the chances for severe weather near those dates.

March 3

The first days of March often bring a false sense of spring to much of the nation. In an average year, the March 3rd front is often relatively gentle, prolonging the opportunities for tapping trees and doing other outdoor work. But lunar perigee on March 3rd this year could bring a blustery start of the month.

March 5

Precipitation and wind typically mark this second March front, and the last major snowstorm of the first half of the year sometimes strikes the Middle Atlantic region.

After this front passes through, farmers along the Pacific coast typically begin planting their spring barley. Throughout most of the nation, the passage of this front coincides with spring soil testing and the addition of fertilizer to pastures.

March 9

The March 9th front is the most dangerous and the coldest high-pressure system in the first two-thirds of March. Be ready to protect young lambs and kids from hypothermia. Full moon on the 12th is likely to intensify weather conditions related to both this front and the next.

March 14

Throughout the Deep South, the passage of the relatively benign pre-equinox weather system signals the start of planting sweet corn and corn for grain. In Texas and Arizona, farmers put in cotton.

March 19

The equinox front historically brings freezing temperatures and clear skies to the northern half of the nation. On the other hand, lunar apogee on the 18th may bring slightly milder temperatures this year.

March 24

The March 24th system is usually less powerful than the fronts that precede and follow it. This year's new moon on the 27th, however, could chill outdoor activities.

March 29

Warm weather at the approach of this system is associated with thunderstorms and tornadoes. Be ready to protect livestock in the event of violent weather. New moon on the 27th and lunar perigee on the 30th increase the chances for stormy weather.

For all its dangers, however, the last front of March brings middle spring, the period during which almost all the field crops are planted, most of the lambs, kids and calves are moved to pasture, and flowering trees and bulbs are everywhere.

Almanack Phenology: When...Then

When pussy willows emerge all the way, that is a sign that maple syrup time is just about over for the year and that red-winged blackbirds have started to stake out their territories.

When maples flower and woodchucks dig up the hillsides, then onion sets can be tucked into the garden soil.

When coltsfoot buds in the hills of Pennsylvania and West Virginia, azaleas are past their prime in Georgia.

When aspens bloom in the Rocky Mountains, watch grizzly bears emerge from hibernation.

When bleeding hearts are an inch tall, then purple cress blooms in the bottomlands.

When bumblebees and carpenter bees work in the flowers, then it's time for termites (looking like flying ants) to swarm.

Cabbage butterflies announce that bass and sunfish are moving to spawn in shallow waters.

When you see golden forsythia flowering, then you know that middle spring has come to your township, and that the first major wave of wildflowers, including the trilliums and bloodroots and

Dutchman's britches, will be in bloom throughout the woods.

When the rhubarb is up a few inches, then the daffodils are blooming.

When raspberry and rose bushes develop fresh leaves and wild onions are getting lanky, then bald eagle chicks hatch and peregrine falcons lay their eggs.

When box elders bloom and pussy willow catkins get their pollen, then the first mosquitoes bite.

When magnolias bloom in the Ohio valley, then Sandhill cranes are migrating in the Rocky Mountains.

When the mourning cloaks, the question marks and the tortoise shell butterflies come out, catfish are feeding and goldfinches are turning gold.

When you see the first monarch butterflies in your garden, and the iris start to bud, that's the time to go out to the fields looking for armyworms, slugs, corn borers, flea beetles and leafhoppers.

When you hear the robin chorus an hour or so before dawn, then look for green-bottle flies and garter snakes.

A Floating Calendar of Bloom for Wildflowers, Perennials, Shrubs and Trees

March 3:	**Baby Blue Eyes (nemophila)**
March 4:	**Chickweed (stellaria media)**

March 5:	Small-Flowered Bittercress (cardamine parviflora)
March 8:	Snow Trillium (trillium nivale)
March 9:	Purple Deadnettle (lamium purpureum)
March 10:	Mid-Season Crocus
March 11:	Dandelion (taraxacum)
March 12:	Scilla (scilla siberica)
March 15:	Early Daffodils (narcissus)
March 23:	Hepatica (hepatica Americana)
	Dutchman's Britches (dicentra cucullaria)
March 24:	Periwinkle (vinca major)
	Cornus Mas
March 25:	Violet Cress (Cochlearia acaulis)
	Lesser Celandine (ranunculus ficaria)
March 26:	Lungwort (pulmonaria)
March 28:	Bloodroot (sanguinaria canadensis)
	Spicebush (lindera benzoin)
March 29:	Spring Beauty (claytonia)
March 30:	Twinleaf (Jeffersonia diphylla)
March 31:	Virginia Bluebell (mertensia Virginica)

Peak Activity Times for Creatures

The following guide to lunar position shows when the moon is above (Best times) or below (Second-best times) the country, the periods during which livestock, people, fish and game are typically the most active and the hungriest.

Date	Best	Second-Best
March 1 – 4:	Afternoons	Midnight to Dawn
March 5 – 11:	Evenings	Mornings
March 12 – 19:	Midnight to Dawn	Afternoons
March 20 – 26:	Mornings	Evenings
March 27 – 31:	Afternoons	Midnight to Dawn

Almanack Literature
Help! What Do I Do?
by Nancy Minor, Bergheim, Texas

We have a young female Border Collie who loves her lambs. Although we gave her the grand name of Tay, we've always called her Tater, which more clearly reflects her personality. Often intimidated by the older ewes, she decided that she would prefer to work only with the lambs, gently herding them in the pen and carefully guarding them in the field.

One day last year, Tater was called upon to perform a duty above and beyond her job description. A ewe with twins had left the pen and walked up the hill leading to the pasture, taking only one twin with her. As she reached the pasture, the ewe called out to her lambs to come and nurse. The twin, who had been daydreaming and had been left behind, started up the hill toward the sound her mother's voice.

At that moment, Tater started

walking down the hill. As the lamb approached her, Tater stopped, and the lamb, not seeing her mother but hearing her voice, approached Tater and started to nuzzle under her back leg, looking for milk. Tater froze and looked at me with such pleading in her eyes, as if she were trying to ask me, "Help! What do I do?"

I was trying so hard not to laugh that I couldn't give a command. So Tater dutifully lifted her back leg for the lamb to nurse. At this point, the lamb realized there was no milk to be had and jumped back, mortified I'm sure, to be caught nursing on a dog.

APRIL
2017

Vivir es ver volver:

To live is to see each thing return.

Azorín

The Gregorian Calendar for April

S	M	T	W	T	F	S
						1
2	3	4	5	6	7	8
9	10	11	12	13	14	15
16	17	18	19	20	21	22
23	24	25	26	27	28	29
30						

The Ecliptic of Middle Spring

In early April mornings, Hercules has moved to near the center of the sky over Ophiuchus, Libra and Scorpio. The Summer Triangle, which includes Cygnus, Lyra and Aquila, is just a little behind him in the east. The Milky Way passes through the Triangle, blending it with autumn's Pegasus rising. The Corona Borealis has shifted into the western heavens, and the pointers of the Big Dipper point almost exactly east-west.

Parallel to these and other celestial forms are constellations of objects close at hand: flowers and birds and amphibians and mammals. Throughout the many brief sub-seasons of the year, such creatures reflect the tilt and the spin of Earth.

Earth star clusters of plants and animals, like asterisms made up of distant objects, are fabrications that create seasonal time.

And so after a walk in the woods, one might imagine a Spring Triangle formation made up of red toad trilliums and golden cowslip and bluebells.

Or maybe a Libra-like cluster with four corners: goldfinches in April plumage, bloodroot, morning robinsong, and screeching, mating toads.

Or a lopsided, six-pointed, Cepheus-like collection of honking geese and watercress and the first pale spikes of lizard's tail, the flushed, red bellies of young river chubs, the fattening skunk cabbage leaves and the whistle of red-winged blackbirds.

Or a nine-piece Aquila-like fantasy of daffodils, tulips, serviceberry flowers, pear flowers, wind flowers, buttercups, creeping phlox and new wisteria.

Or a gangly Ophiuchus-like sprawl of morels and cardinals, trout lilies and redbuds, peaches and crab apples, hyacinths, violets and vast patches of dandelions.

In fact, the land of middle spring (like the land of all the other seasons) is an immediate and immanent ecliptic full of bright, soft, fragrant, fair and vociferous constellations. Along its cosmic band lie signs under which to pluck a treasure of astrological fortune, riches from the neighborhood instead of from galaxies far away.

The Apple Blossom Moon and the Mock Orange Moon

As middle spring deepens, more and more trees come into bloom: the plums, the apples and the peaches and the pears and so many more. Forsythia flowers in the hedgerows, and the Great Violet and Dandelion Bloom begins. Then mock orange shrubs release the deepest scent of spring, foretelling peonies and iris and lilacs.

April 3: The moon enters its second quarter at 1:39 p.m.

April 11: The Apple Blossom Moon is full at 1:08 a.m.

April 15: Lunar apogee (when the moon is farthest from Earth)

April 19: The moon enters its final phase at 4:57 a.m.

April 26: The Mock Orange Moon is new at 7:16 a.m.

April 27: Lunar perigee (when the moon is closest to Earth)

The S.A.D. Stress Index

April brings the day's length and the chances for mild weather into single digits on the S.A.D. Stress Index scale. Only the cloud column holds out at March levels, but that is not enough to keep the Index from dipping into the gentle 20s.

Totals of 75 to 65: Severe Stress
64 to 50: Severe to moderate stress
49 to 35: Moderate stress
34 to 25: Light to moderate stress
24 and below: No stress

Day	Clouds	Weather	Daylight	Totals
April 1:	16	11	10	37
April 15:	14	8	9	31
April 30:	12	7	7	26

The Sun

Cross-Quarter Day is April 21, halfway between equinox and solstice, and the Sun enters the late spring sign of Taurus on the same date.

The meager inventories of change that characterize equinox now quickly fill with new details each day. The floral and faunal fragments of the season multiply, literally filling in the space of Earth with tangible, visible clockwork.

The Planets

♃ ♄ ♂ ♀

Venus in Pisces is the bright morning star, low in the east before dawn. Mars moves retrograde once again, its red glow complementing the scarlet eye of Taurus along the western horizon after dark. Jupiter, remaining in Virgo, lies close to the western horizon before dawn, at its brightest (and its moons most visible) on April 7. Saturn, in Sagittarius, moves above the southern horizon as the Sun brightens the east.

The Stars

Late in the evening, look for the twins of Gemini above you in the western half of the sky. A little farther west, almost directly above Orion, the brightest star is Capella. Along the southwestern horizon, the most prominent star is Sirius, the Dog Star of middle summer

Before sunrise, Hercules has moved to near the center of the sky. The Summer Triangle, which includes bright Vega, Altair, and Deneb, is just a little behind Hercules to his east. The Milky Way passes through the triangle, separating it from autumn's Pegasus rising on the eastern horizon. The Corona Borealis has shifted into the western half of the heavens, and the pointers of the Big Dipper point almost exactly east-west.

The Shooting Stars

The Lyrid Meteors are active after midnight between Cygnus and Hercules during the second and third week of April, peaking on April 22 and 23. These shooting stars often appear at the rate of 15 to 25 per hour.

Calendar of Feast Days and Holidays for Farmers, Gardeners and Homesteaders

April 1 – June 15, 2017: Plan ahead to serve the graduation cookout market – college graduations can start as early as the first week in April and extend into the middle of June.

April 10 (sunset) – April 18, 2017: Passover: The Jewish market typically is best after religious holidays come to a close. Milk-fed lambs and kids below 60 pounds are favored for the Passover market. Lamb stew is a traditional Seder dish at Passover Seder dinners.

April 13 – 15, 2017: New Year's Day for immigrants from Cambodia, Thailand and Laos. The Asian market often favors animals in the 70-pound live-weight range.

April 16, 2017: Roman Easter and Orthodox Easter: Save your newly weaned, milk-fed lambs and kids, weighing about 25 to 45 pounds and not older than three months, for this market. Light-colored meat is best, a sign of the suckling animal. Orthodox Easter animals should also be milk fed. They can be a little bit bigger than the Roman Easter lambs or kids (between 40 and 60 pounds.

Farming and Gardening With the Moon

After the first cold wave of April moves east and the moon is waxing, farmers and gardeners throughout the central areas of the United States typically plant their sweet corn and their head lettuce.

April under the waxing moon is a fine time to plant late summer and autumn grasses and legumes in order to extend your grazing season. Plant rice and cotton in the South, spring grains, along the Canadian border, soybeans in Mississippi, sugar beets in the Midwest.

Early April frosts can cut into the availability of pollen for bees and other insects. If bees are not bringing in pollen, feed a pollen substitute.

The Moon and the Weather

Weather history indicates that cold waves will cross the Mississippi around the dates listed below. The fronts pass through the West 24 to 48 hours prior to their arrival in the Midwest; they reach the East 24 to 48 hours later.

Major storms are most likely to occur on the days between April 1 and 11 and April 19 through the 27. Full moon on the 11th and new moon on the 26th (and perigee on the 27th) are likely to encourage frost above the 35th Parallel.

April 2

Since this front, like the March 29th front, is associated with high winds and lightning, continue to keep an eye out for conditions that would threaten your animals and your family.

April 6

The April 6th front is often a treacherous weather system, bringing warm winds prior to its arrival, then burning the flowers of apples, pears and peaches after it passes through.

April 11

Although this is usually a relatively mild "sandwich front," nestled between the April 6th system and the wet and windy April 16th front, this year's full moon on the 11th is likely to intensify this weather system

Throughout the country, the normal average air temperature rises at the rate of about one degree every three days once the April 11th front passes through (and the moon wanes). And the field and garden day is increasing at an average rate of two minutes per day.

April 16

Precipitation typically occurs as this front races across the United States. After the front passes, however, expect warm weather to nurture your early April plantings. Lunar apogee on the 15th is likely to increase chances for mild temperatures.

April 21

Chances for snow and frost in the Midwest recede quickly after this front comes through. Winds and hard rain, however, continue to threaten young plantings, kids, lambs and calves.

April 24

The odds for outstanding field and garden weather improve immensely after the passage of this front. Seed all the rest of your flowers and vegetables in flats or directly in the garden. Even in the northern tier of states, the danger of frost gradually becomes quite low as May approaches. Throughout the Deep South, farmers can even plant tender peanuts. Be careful of new moon time on the 26th, however. It will carry the chance of frost down to the Border States.

April 28

Warm and wet weather is associated with this front, and lunar perigee on the 27th increases the chances for precipitation. Have the field and garden ready to take advantage of this moisture window. This is especially important in the event of a dry May or a wet, cold May that can delay sprouting.

Almanack Phenology: When... Then

When nettles are six inches tall, then middle spring wildflowers are open in the woods.

When you hear the shrill call of the American toad, that will be the time to plant all your corn.

Look for morel mushrooms when May apples push out from the ground and cowslip buds in the swamp. That's when leaves come out on skunk cabbage.

Parsnips in bloom will tell you that deer are growing their new antlers and all the rest of your garden weeds are coming in.

When you see the high canopy budding and greening, listen for wild turkeys to be gobbling.

When tulips flower in the garden; they tell you about the turkeys, too, and they also remind you to mow the lawn before it gets too long.

Or if you have no tulips but are mowing the lawn anyway (or don't want to mow it), the long grass will tell you that opossums and raccoons are giving birth in the woodlot and young goslings are hatching in the ponds and rivers.

When you see tent caterpillars in the trees and the redbuds starting to turn purple, stop and search for tadpoles in the ponds.

Then it won't be long before dogwoods and the crab apples open, and winter grains are almost tall enough to ripple in the wind.

When the pussy willow bushes start to get their leaves, meadowlarks and scarlet tanagers return for summer.

When chicory is nine inches high,

rhubarb is ready for pie, and hops vines crawl all over the garden.

When you pick your first strawberry in Missouri, then you know peonies are budding in Iowa and that privets are getting leaves in Louisville.

As soon as you see hummingbird moths at the new flowers, you may start sneezing because all the trees and grasses are coming into bloom.

When the great annual dandelion flowering begins, then snakehead mushrooms appear.

When ticks and mosquitoes appear, the morel season is about over, and the last frost is only four weeks away.

When the clovers bloom, flea season begins for pets and livestock, and flies take over the barn.

When wisteria comes into flower, the most fragrant time of year is here. Lilacs, mock orange and honeysuckle follow the wisteria.

When you see admiral butterflies, that means buckeye trees will bloom

And when garlic mustard flowers in the woods, cutworms and sod webworms start taking over the field and garden. Weevils are showing up in the alfalfa, too.

A Floating Calendar of Bloom for Wildflowers, Weeds, Garden Perennials, Shrubs and Trees

April 1:	Grape Hyacinth (muscari armeniacum)
	Purple deadnettle (lamium purpureum)
	Taxus (taxus)
	Field Peppergrass (lepidium campestre)
April 2:	Ground Ivy (glechoma hederacea)
	Forsythia (forsythia)
	Box Elder (acer negundo)
April 3:	Small-Flowered Buttercup (ranunculus abortivus)
	Creeping Phlox (phlox subulata)
April 4:	Swamp Buttercup (ranunculus septentrionalis)
	Serviceberry (amelanchier)
	Scilla (scilla siberica)
	Shepherd's Purse (capsella pursa-pastoris)
April 5:	Wood Hyacinth (hyacinthoides hispanica)
	Puschkinia (puschkinia libanotica)
April 6:	Dwarf Plum (prunus domestica)
	Red Maple (acer rubrum)
	Wind Flower (anemone nemorosa)
	Rue Anemone (thalictrum thalictroides)
April 7:	Purple Violet (viola papilionacea)
	Toad Trillium (trillium sessile)
	Star Magnolia (magnolia stellate)
April 8:	Red-Flowered Quince (chaenomelesspeciosa)
April 9:	Early Season Tulip (tulipa)
	Fritillary (fritillaria)
April 10:	Cowslip (primula veris)
	Decorative Pear (pyrus calleryana)
	Ash (fraxinus)
	Sugar Maple (acer saccharum)
April 11:	Crabapple (malus)

Cherry (prunus cerasus)
Peach (prunus persica)
Bleeding Heart (lamprocapnos
    spectabilis)
Blue Cohosh (caulophyllum
    thalictroides)

April 12: Mid-Season Daffodils (narcissus)
Bluettes (houstonia caerulea)

April 13: Wisteria (wisteria frutescens)
Bellwort (uvularia)
Hawthorn (crataegus monogyna)
Pink Magnolia (magnolia soulangeana)

April 14: Large-flowered Trillium (trillium
    grandiflorum)
Winter Cress (barbarea)
Jacob's Ladder (polemonium
    caeruleum)

April 15: Redbud (cercis canadensis)
Mid-Season Tulip (tulipa)
Trout Lily (erythronium americanum)

April 16: Domestic Strawberry (fragaria
    ananassa)
Pink Magnolia (magnolia liliiflora)
White Violet (viola Canadensis)

April 17: Buttercup (ranunculus)
Money Plant (epipremnum aureum)
Thyme-Leafed Speedwell (veronica
    serpyllifolia)

April 19: Dogwood (cornus)
Blue Speedwell (veronica)
Watercress (nasturtium officinale)

April 20: Lilac (syringa)
Raspberry (rubus idaeus)
Ragwort (jacobaea vulgaris)

April 21: Snowball Viburnum: (viburnum   ``
    macrocephalum)
Azalea (rhododendron indicum)
Early Meadow Rue (thalictrum
    Dioicum)
Columbine (aquilegia vulgaris)

April 22: Bridal Wreath Spirea (spirea
    prunifolia)
Late-Season Tulips and Daffodils

April 23: Wild Geranium (geranium maculatum)

Miterwort (mitella)
Wild Phlox (phlox divaricate)
Celandine (stylophorum diphyllum)
April 24: Clematis (clematis x jackmanii)
Wood Hyacinth (hyacinthoides non-
    scripta)
Garlic Mustard (alliaria petiolata)
April 25: Jack-in-the-Pulpit (arisaema
    triphyllum)
Wild Ginger (asarum caudatum)
April 26: Meadow Parsnip (haspium trifoliatum)
Wood Betony (stachys officinalis)
Honeysuckle (lonicera tatarica L.)
Buckeye (aesculus glabra)
Red Horse-Chestnut (aesculus carnea)
Nodding Trillium (trillium cernuum)
Star of Bethlehem (ornithogalum
    narbonense)
April 27: Early-Season Iris (iridaceae)
Thyme (thymus vulgaris)
Horseradish (armoracia rusticana)
Common Fleabane (erigeron)
April 28: Osage Orange (maclura pomifera)
Lily-of-the-Valley (convallaria majalis)
April 29: Wild Cherry (prunus avium)
Spring Cress (cardamine)
April 30: Sweet William (dianthus barbatus)
Korean Lilac (syringa meyeri)
Catchweed (galium aparine)
Larkspur (delphinium carolinianum)

Peak Activity Times for Creatures

The following guide to lunar position shows when the moon is above (Best times) or below (Second-best times) the country, and, therefore, the periods during which livestock, people, fish and game are typically the most active and the hungriest.

Date	Best	Second-Best
April 1 – 2:	Afternoons	Midnight to Dawn
April 3 – 10:	Evenings	Mornings
April 11 – 18:	Midnight to Dawn	Afternoons
April 19 – 25:	Mornings	Evenings
April 26 – 30:	Afternoons	Midnight to Dawn

Almanack Literature
Way Back Then:
Summers on the Farm
by Charles Sutton, North Clarendon, Vermont

For many summers when I was in high school or college just after WWII, I worked on a small dairy farm not far from home.

The owner, James Nason, was "a gentleman farmer." During the week he commuted to New York City where he had a top position with an advertising firm. He had three daughters — Jane, Carol and Sarah — any one of whom my parents had hoped either my brother Fred or I would someday marry. Never happened even though I did time on the dance floor with Carol as urged by my parents.

Jim, as he liked to be called by us farm hands — two to four teenagers plus farm manager Dick Dunton — enjoyed being with us working the farm as often as he could, riding the Farmall tractor or a small bulldozer.

The farm included a dozen or so Guernsey cows and a large flock of chickens. There would sometimes be a horse or two, which his daughters looked after.

The Nasons had many friends including my parents who bought their milk, cream, butter, chickens and eggs, which were delivered by Dick to our homes.

We farm hands helped with the milking, pasteurizing and bottling the milk and cream, looked after the chickens from chicks to egg making or meat, and did the haying. This being an estate, we cut the grass and attended the gardens, and cleaned an in-ground swimming pool.

I also learned how to process chickens: killing, defeathering them with a chicken plucking machine and eviscerating or dressing them out. Dick decided not to teach me how to caponize roosters, much to my relief. I'll never forget my first week there, a time when "the rookie" had to be broken in.

One of my very first jobs was to scrape the cows' bottoms which were always caked dirty especially when the cows started eating spring green grasses. I passed that test and went on to the next.

I was excited about learning to drive the tractor and using its immense forklift. One day my fellow workers asked if I would like to hook up the manure spreader and do its job on a field. The spreader was filled with moist cow plops from the barn and chicken manure, which we collected daily from drop trays beneath their roosts.

My first run down the field went fine, but on the return trip this "rookie" was taught a lesson. I didn't realize it was so windy. Soon I was also spread with the bits and chunks of manure riding out the wind. The other farm hands thought this was pretty funny.

But the experience had a happy ending. We who looked after a large in-ground pool were allowed to have a quick dip there in the late afternoon provided we showered first and got out before our boss Jim got home. And when Jim did get home he would invite us into his office in the barn to offer us a drink of beer or whiskey. Pretty grown-up stuff for teenage boys!

MAY
2017

Onward and nearer rides the sun of May;
And wide around, the marriage of the plants
Is sweetly solemnized. Then flows amain
The surge of summer's beauty; dell and crag,
Hollow and lake, hillside and pine arcade,
Are touched with genius.

Ralph Waldo Emerson, "Musketaquid"

The Gregorian Calendar for May

S	M	T	W	T	F	S
	1	2	3	4	5	6
7	8	9	10	11	12	13
14	15	16	17	18	19	20
21	22	23	24	25	26	27
28	29	30	31			

Spring Soul

On a trip last spring to the Museum of Glass in Corning, New York, I saw a small figurine: a prone girl of raku-fired ceramic, a glass replica of her rising from her waist.

The work was called "While You Were Sleeping," and it was created by Christina Bothwell, a Pennsylvania sculptor. The artist's statement said that the sculpture was "to make visible the idea that we are souls housed in skin bodies." The medium of glass, stated the artist, "holds light in its mass, just as the spirit is held in the physical body."

Even though the piece was perhaps more autumnal than vernal, its effect on me was to make me think of new life rather than of life receding. Instead of the spirit leaving the physical body, it was just as likely entering, allowing itself to be held, willingly being housed.

The idea was certainly not a novel one to me, but it struck me hard, as art can sometimes do, and put me off-balance, revealing to me more powerfully something I thought I already knew. It was, I suppose, the use of transparent glass, which was material but represented spirit, that was, in the hands of Christina Bothwell, equally as credible and as substantial, as the raku ceramic flesh. The truth of the sculpture suddenly converted me, exposing the parity of dimensions.

It immediately brought to mind an incident several years ago in which the spirit of someone very dear to me appeared to a family member. The apparition occurred almost at the moment of her death but several thousand miles away from where she lay.

"Look at my beautiful new body!" the spirit exclaimed, happy, glowing, shining. Indeed, I was told, the form was of exceptional elegance. She went on to describe the freedom and the joy that she felt and how she would always be with the ones she loved.

And so I was reminded by the encounter in the museum of the correspondence between spirit and form, and of how events in nature are hardly what they seem, and that new life in springtime is not simply some elusive invigoration of matter (be it in hepatica or daffodil, tree or fledgling or human) but a mirror of the outward shape as well as an infusion of the mass of soul, which, except for its medium, is identical to (if not even more glorious than) everything in the tangible object.

The Mock Orange Moon and the Strawberry and Raspberry Moon

Late spring is the most fragrant time of the year in many yards, under the power of Japanese honeysuckle, peonies and mock orange. In this sweetest season, strawberries ripen, and raspberries and blackberries flower to promise summer.

May 2: The moon enters its second quarter at 9:42 p.m.
May 10: The Mock Orange Moon is full at 4:42 p.m.
May 12: Lunar apogee (when the moon is farthest from Earth)
May 18: The moon enters its final quarter at 7:33 p.m.
May 25: The Strawberry and Raspberry Moon is new at 2:44 p.m.
May 26: Lunar perigee (when the moon is closest to Earth)

The S.A.D. Stress Index

May brings an easing of seasonal affective disorder for the majority of people in the Northern Hemisphere. The summer-like day's length, the gentle weather of spring, and the gradually decreasing cloud cover, contribute to the start of the least stressful period of the year.

Key for Interpreting the S.A.D. Index:
Totals of_75 to 65: S.A.D. Alert: Severe Stress for those who suffer from seasonal affective disorders
64 to 50: Severe to moderate stress
49 to 35: Moderate stress
34 to 25: Light to moderate stress

24 and below: Light stress

Day	Clouds	Weather	Daylight	Totals
May 1:	11	7	7	25
May 20:	8	5	3	16
May 31:	6	4	0	10

The Sun

On May 9, the sun reaches three-fourths of the way to summer solstice. Between this date and August 5, the northern hemisphere enjoys the longest and sunniest days of the year.

The Sun enters the early summer sign of Gemini on May 21.

The Planets

♃ ♄ ♂ ♀

Venus continues to ride Pisces as the morning star in the east. Mars keeps its position in Taurus, close to the western horizon at dusk, almost touching red Aldebaran on May 7 (Aldebaran being the twinkling red object). Jupiter, visible in the west after midnight, disappears from view before the sun comes up. Still in Sagittarius, Saturn can be found along the southern horizon after midnight.

The Stars

Cassiopeia and the Milky Way lie on the northern horizon in the late evening. Cygnus rises from the northeast, Ophiuchus from the east, Sagittarius and Libra from the southeast. Centaurus and Corvus are low on the southern horizon. Hydra snakes across the southwest. Monoceros is setting in the west, Capella and Perseus disappearing into the northwest.

The Shooting Stars

The Eta Aquarids are active on the 5th and 6th of May, but only a few meteors per hour occur with this shower, and those will be obscured by the bright, gibbous moon.

Calendar of Feast Days and Holidays for Farmers, Gardeners and Homesteaders

May 14, 2017: Mother's Day

May 27, 2017: Ramadan begins at sunset on the 27th. Now is the time to advertise your farm to the Halal market in preparation for the close of Ramadan on June 25th.

May 29, 2017: Memorial Day

Farming and Gardening with the Moon

The waxing moon and rising soil temperatures this late spring invite commercial cabbage planting across the North and completion of the planting of oats and other spring grains in the central states. Orchard grass will be heading below the Border States. Asparagus is fresh for cutting as it shoots up in the sun throughout the northern states.

Typically, the first half of May is better than the second half for fieldwork. Across the South, haying is in full swing in anticipation of wetter weather toward the end of the month. And strawberry time spreads North at the same rate as that of spring, bringing in the sweet, red berries all the way from Arkansas to Tennessee and the Carolinas.

The Strawberry Rains, however, often complicate berry time, and clouds and precipitation sometimes remain through the end of May, the stagnation reflecting a general slowdown in the conflict between spring and summer. Although fields planted prior to late-May rains are almost sure to sprout now, cool and damp conditions can stunt growth in soggy fields.

Weaker animals (and people, too) are especially vulnerable to disease during these damp days. Parasites thrive in the moisture; pasture plants can have an unusually high water content, and livestock may not get enough nutrition from this forage. Silage and hay supplements can take up the feeding slack. Keep salt available for your animals, too; it will help to prevent bloat.

In the West, winter rains are ordinarily over by the middle of late spring, signaling the beginning of shearing season. (The waning moon favors that!)

In the northern tier of states, frost is still possible on or about new moon day, but the danger is not severe enough to halt the annual seeding of sunflowers throughout the sunflower belt.

The third week of May usually means that insects reach the economic threshold all across the central United States, and the new moon combined with perigee this year is likely to encourage more insect activity.

The dark moon toward the end of this May favors the performance of animal maintenance. And if you set out your commercial and home garden tomatoes now, they should be relatively safe from freezing temperatures. The dark moon will promote root development (if the ground is not too wet).

The Moon and the Weather

Weather history indicates that cold waves will cross the Mississippi around the dates listed below. The fronts pass through the West 24 to 48 hours prior to their arrival in the Midwest; they reach the East 24 to 48 hours later.

Major storms are most likely to occur on the days between May 8 – 14 and May 17 – 23. Full moon on the 10th and new moon on the 25th (along with lunar perigee on the 26th) increase the chances for frost near those dates.

May 2

"Lilac Winter" often arrives with the first days of May, threatening frost in the northern states. This year, however, early May should be produce more benign temperatures under the weak waxing moon.

May 7

Mild days between the first and second May fronts bring out the tomato and bean plants to the garden, but watch for frost between the 8th and the 12th, the days around full moon.

May 12

Just as tender bedding plants are set out before Mother's Day, the last really dangerous, frost-bearing front of the spring moves across the nation. But two days after the passage of the May 12th cold wave, mild weather often occurs, helping the new seeds to sprout. The waning moon and lunar apogee will encourage your potatoes to develop strong roots; plant soon.

May 15

The Strawberry Rains often follow the arrival of the May 15th cool front (and the ripening of strawberries in the southern and central states).

May 20

The Strawberry Rains may continue to plague pastures and hay fields as this front approaches, but plan to make the first cut of alfalfa along the 40th Parallel after the high-pressure system comes through.

May 24

New moon on the 25th and lunar perigee on the 26th combine to threaten frost across the northern tier of states and at higher elevations. Gradually rising temperatures will soon be having an effect on the amount of food your livestock will need, since metabolic rate rises with the thermometer.

Almanack Phenology: When...Then

When you see lamb's ear, tea roses, pink spirea or privets blooming, then you can plant your tomatoes with hardly a thought for a damaging freeze (but keep protection handy).

When daisies flower by the wayside and white mulberries and mountain maples bloom, then find daddy longlegs in the undergrowth and darners by the water's edge.

When redbud trees get seedpods in Indiana, then horseshoe crabs mate along the Carolina and Georgia coastline.

When lilac flowers fade, hawthorn lace bugs and hawthorn leafminers emerge in the hawthorns. Pine needle scale eggs, cooley spruce gall adelgid and Eastern spruce gall adelgid eggs hatch, too.

When poppies bloom, white-throated

sparrows, ruby-crowned kinglets, yellow-rumped warblers, magnolia warblers, tanagers, grosbeaks and orioles migrate.

When tulips are in full bloom in the North, the best of the spring wildflowers have all disappeared in the Southwest. But you can still find prickly pear cacti flowering in the desert.

When mock orange reaches full flower, look for black vine weevils and greater peach tree borers. Then come the rhododendron borers and the dogwood borers!

When the great spring dandelion bloom reaches into the Northeast, pelicans and trumpeter swans lay eggs near Yellowstone Lake, and gosling hatch all along the Mississippi.

When multiflora roses come into flower, the bronze birch borer emerges and oystershell scale eggs hatch.

When American holly blooms (about the same time as the multiflora roses), then potato leafhoppers will be hopping in the potatoes.

When hummingbirds arrive at your feeders, look for thrushes, catbirds and scarlet tanagers to arrive, too.

When strawberries come into full bloom, wild cucumber sprouts along the fencerows.

When summer phlox are two-feet tall, listen for catbirds in the bushes,

When apple blossoms fall, the rare, medicinal golden seal blooms in the woods.

When you see mayflies by the water, spitbugs make their spittle shelters in the parsnips, and the first cut of hay is underway.

When chives bloom in the garden, then crappie fishing peaks in the shallows.

When flower clusters of the sweet-gum tree fall, check to see if your first strawberry is red.

When azaleas lose their petals, swallowtail butterflies come looking for flowers.

When flea beetles feed in the vegetable garden and cedar waxwings migrate into the North, then fiddler crabs emerge from their tunnels in the estuaries of the South.

When the last locust flowers fall to the ground, then mulberries ripen. In the wetlands, the wild iris blooms.

When you see cottonwood cotton in the wind, then deer will be giving birth and pollen from grasses will be reaching its peak. Panicled dogwood will be budding, and grackles will be feeding their pesky young.

When blackberries have set fruit across the South, then sunflowers are in full bloom in southern California, and spring wheat and oats are just about all planted in the North. .

When Canadian thistles start to bud, it's safe to plant peppers, cantaloupes and cucumbers.

When the first thistle blooms, the corn should be at least eight inches tall.

When you hear spring crickets sing, look for leafhoppers in the garden and snapping turtle eggs in the sand.

A Floating Calendar of Bloom for Wildflowers, Weeds, Garden Perennials, Shrubs and Trees

May 1:	**Silver Olive (elaeagnus angustifolia)**
	Sweet Gum (liquidambar styraciflua)
	Comfrey (symphytum officinale)
	Spring Sedum (sedum ternatum)
May 2:	**Poppy (papaver somniferum)**
	English Daisy (bellis perennis)
May 3:	**White Mulberry (morus alba)**
	Mountain Maple (acer spicatum)
May 4:	**Black Locust (robinia pseudoacacia)**
	Honey locust (gleditsia triacanthos)
	Black Walnut (juglans nigra)
	Oaks (quercus)
	Wood Sorrel (oxalis acetosella)
May 5:	**Painted daisy: Pyrethrum (pyrethrum roseum)**
	Golden Alexander (zizia aurea)
	May Apple (podophyllum peltatum)
	Hawthorn (crataegus monogyna)
May 6:	**Rhododendron (rhododendron)**
	Columbine (aquilegia)
May 7:	**Sweet Cicely (myrrhis odorata)**
	Robin's Fleabane (erigeron pulchellus)
	English Plantain (plantago lanceolata)
May 8:	**Mock Orange (philadelphus coronaries)**

	Sweet William (dianthus barbatus)
	Shooting Star (dodecatheon)
May 9:	**Chives (allium schoenoprasum)**
	Catmint (nepeta)
	Waterleaf (talinum fruticosum)
	Wild Raspberry (rubus idaeus)
May 10:	**Sweet Rocket Dame's Rocket (hesperis matronalis)**
	Dwarf Larkspur (delphinium tricorne)
	Tulip Tree (liriodendro)
	Yellowwood (cladrastis kentukea)
	Snow-on-the-Mountain (euphorbia marginata)
May 11:	**Elm (ulmus)**
	Chamomile (matricaria chamomilla)
May 12:	**Clustered Snakeroot (sanicula gregaria)**
	White Clover (trifolium repens)
	Meadow Goat's Beard (tragopogon dubius)
	Red Clover (trifolium pretense)
May 13:	**Common Plantain (plantago major)**
	Black Medic (medicago lupulina)
	Wild Multiflora Rose (rosa multiflora)
	Blue Flag (iris versicolor)
	Wild Daisy (bellis perennis)
May 14:	**Wild Mallow (malva sylvestris)**
	Spiderwort (tradescantia)
	Scabiosa (scabiosa)
	Lupine (lupines)
	Geum (geum abendsonne)
	Baneberry (actaea)
	Fire Pink (silene virginica)
May 15:	**Common Orange Day Lily (hemerocallis fulva)**
	Stella d'Oro Lily (hemerocallis 'Stella de Oro')
May 16:	**Yucca (yucca filamentosa)**
	Blue Flax (linum lewisii)
	Foxglove (digitalis purpurea)
	Blackberry (rubus villosus)
May 17:	**Achillea (achillea millefolium)**
	Swamp Iris (iris)
	Wild Grape (vitis vinifera)
	Cow Vetch (vicia villosa)

	Peonies (paeonia)
May 18:	Lamb's Ear (stachys byzantine)
	Kousa Dogwood (cornus kousa)
	Yellow Sweet Clover (melilotus officinalis)
May 19:	Climbing Rose (rosa setigera)
	Tea Rose (rosoideae rosa)
	Fringe Tree (chionanthus)
May 20:	Blue-Eyed Grass (sisyrinchium angustifolium)
	Corn Salad (valerianella locusta)
May 21:	Catalpa (catalpa speciosa)
	Pink Spirea (spiraea japonica)
	Wild Parsnip (pastinaca sativa)
May 22:	Privet (ligustrum)
	River Willow (salix myrtilloides)
	Smooth Solomon's Seal (polygonatum biflorum)
May 23:	Astilbe (astilbe arendsii)
	Panicled Dogwood (cornus racemosa)
	Poison Hemlock (conium maculatum)
	Angelica (angelica sp)
	Birdsfoot Trefoil (lobus corniculatus)
May 24:	Japanese Honeysuckle (lonicera japonica)
	Motherwort (leonurus cardiac)
	Multiflora Rose (rosa multifora)
May 25:	Tree of Heaven (ailanthus altissima)
	Yarrow (achillea mullefolium)
	Curly Dock (rumex crispus)
May 26:	Poison Ivy (toxicosdendron radicans)
	White Campion (silene latifolia)
	Common Cinquefoil (potentilla simplex)
May 27:	Cottonwood (aigeiros)
	Honewort (cryptotaenia canadensis)
	Japanese Pond Iris (iris versicolor)
May 28:	Elderberry (sambucus)
	Lesser Stitchwort (stellaria graminea)
May 29:	Lychnis (lychnis coronaria)
	Cow Parsnip (heracleum)
May 30:	Canadian Thistle (cirsium arvense)
May 31:	Catalpa (catalpa speciosa)
	Coreopsis (coreopsis lanceolata)

Chicory (cichorium intybus)
Daisy Fleabane (erigeron annus)

Peak Activity Times for Creatures

The following guide to lunar position shows when the moon is above (Best times) or below (Second-best times) the country, and, therefore, the period during which livestock, people, fish and game are typically the most active and the hungriest.

Date	Best	Second-Best
May 1 – 2:	Afternoons	Midnight to Dawn
May 3 – 9:	Evenings	Mornings
May 11 – 17:	Midnight to Dawn	Afternoons
May 18 – 24:	Mornings	Evenings
May 25 – 30:	Afternoons	Midnight to Dawn

Almanack Literature
The Babysitters' Club
By Patty Greene, Rockville, Indiana

We live on a farm in Parke County, Indiana. We have horses, cows, goats, ducks, geese, peafowl, potbelly pigs, cats and dogs. A normal farm. Maybe.

Last summer, my daughter let her

Nigerian Dwarf goats and their babies out to roam the pastures. When evening came, she went out to put them in the barn away from the harm of coyotes and dogs during the night.

The mama goats came up when she called them, but no babies. Mandy, my daughter, was frantic. Immediately she got her brother to go with her to the back to look for her babies, fearing something had gotten all of them already.

They got to the back pasture and found all the horses in a circle in the very back. When they got closer and continued to call for the babies, the horses looked up but did not move. (You need to understand that this herd of horses contained Percherons, Appaloosas, Quarter Horses, Paints and miniature horses. Quite a mixed group.)

Then, the horses, as a circled group, started moving toward them. There in the middle of the circle of horses were the missing baby goats, safe and sound with their babysitters.

After the horses got the babies to Mandy, they opened up and let the babies go with her to their moms.

JUNE 2017

Our true home is in the present moment. The miracle is not to walk on water. The miracle is to walk on the green earth in the present moment.

Thich Nhat Hahn

The Gregorian Calendar for June

S	M	T	W	T	F	S
				1	2	3
4	5	6	7	8	9	10
11	12	13	14	15	16	17
18	19	20	21	22	23	24
25	26	27	28	29	30	

The Sweetest Way

I have been thinking that if every aspect of the landscape, the immense and long seasons with their untold stages and creatures, if all those things are predetermined by the spin of the Earth and biological clocks, how similar my own changes and progressions must be, all attached to the Sun and the moon, to heat and cold, prearranged as if there were a cosmic map organic to my brain, as though, like some migrating species, I simply did what I needed to do in order to discover and fulfill my purpose.

Such a scenario seems less a deterministic trap or cage than it is a self-guiding pathway: perhaps I do not choose this or that action so much as I evolve to see the sweetest way. Like nature, I am looking for the right signs, for the most fruitful encounter. Like a hiker in the woods, I follow the terrain most in tune with my energy, my sense of adventure, my physical capabilities, my constraints of time. Or, like apple blossoms cede to dogwood and azalea blossoms, so I cede to what comes next in this place. My logic belongs to habitat.

Often it even seems that my whole life has been a preparation for one season or another, and that I know exactly and instinctively what I want or need or must possess. And so what might be called freedom or choice is translated into love or into simple awareness of what is most clearly part of who I am.

And so spring in this place (or in my body) could not, barring some catastrophe, be other than an anteroom to early summer. The land and I do what lies within our sequence, not because we are constrained to do it so much as because it is the only sequence that belongs just to us and into which we fit.

The Strawberry and Raspberry Moon and the Sweet Corn Moon

Strawberries mark the end of late spring, and raspberries pull the year well into early summer. When wild raspberries are sweet, then lilies reach full bloom, orange trumpet creepers send out their flowers, chiggers wander the undergrowth, and the first brood of fledglings have left the nest. In the field and garden, corn sprouts throughout the North and tassels in the South.

June 1: The moon enters its second quarter at 7:42 a.m.
June 8: Lunar apogee (when the moon is farthest from Earth)
June 9: The Strawberry and Raspberry Moon is full at 8:10 a.m.
June 17: The moon enters its final quarter at 6:33 a.m.
June 23: The Sweet Corn Moon is new at 9:31 p.m. and lunar perigee (when the moon is closest to Earth)

June 30: The moon enters its second quarter at 7:51 a.m.

The S.A.D. Stress Index

Unless the weather is unseasonably hot, few people suffer from S.A.D. in June.

Key for Interpreting the S.A.D. Index:
Totals of_75 to 65: S.A.D. Alert: Severe Stress for those who suffer from seasonal affective disorders
64 to 50: Severe to moderate stress
49 to 35: Moderate stress
34 to 25: Light to moderate stress
24 and below: Low Stress

Day	Clouds	Weather	Day	Totals
June 1:	6	3	0	9
June 10:	3	1	0	4
June 15:	1	0	0	1
June 20:	0	5	0	5
June 30:	0	10	0	10

The Sun

June is the year's high tide, the Sun's declination remaining within two degrees of solstice all month. In 2017, the midpoint of the solar year, the day on which the Sun reaches as high in the sky as it will ever go, occurs on June 20 at 11:24 p.m., entering the middle summer sign of Cancer at the same time.

Between June 19 and 23, the sun holds steady at its solstice declination of 23 degrees 26 minutes, and the day's length remains virtually unchanged.

The Planets

♃ ♄ ♂ ♀

Moving retrograde into Aries, Venus keeps its dominant morning place in the eastern sky, reaching its greatest brilliance of the year on June 3. Mars moves retrograde into Gemini but becomes lost in the sunset by the middle of the month; it will not reappear until autumn. Jupiter, traveling deep into the western sky in the evening, disappears with Virgo after midnight. Moving forward into Ophiuchus, Saturn rises after sunset and moves across the sky throughout the night, disappearing well before sunrise.

The Stars

Late in the evening, Arcturus is the brightest star overhead. Libra moves into the far west, Regulus, the star that accompanied early spring daffodils, leading the way. In the northern sky, the Big Dipper lies almost directly above the northern hemisphere, while in the east, Hercules chases the Corona Borealis, and the constellations of the Summer Triangle are rising.

Calendar of Feast Days and Holidays for Farmers, Gardeners and Homesteaders

June 18, 2017: Father's Day

June 25, 2017: Id al Fitr (The Festival of the breaking of the Ramadan Fast): Sheep and goats for this market should not be older than a year. Castrated or uncastrated males are acceptable, as are ewes and does.

Farming and Gardening with the Moon

The power of the Strawberry Rains is usually weakening by now, and relatively stable early-summer weather, combined with the waxing moon, creates a favorable time for putting in the last of the field and garden seeds.

As summer heat builds up, watch for screw worm and blow fly eggs in sores or dung locks on your livestock.

Timely clipping, shearing and dipping can help keep your animals from these pests as well as from ticks, lice and scab mites.

Throughout the month, fertilize asparagus and rhubarb as their seasons end. Side-dress the corn, cut summer cabbage and broccoli. Gather up all the starchy peas, and compost the vines.

Pick summer blueberries as they darken this month. (Very often berries are fattest at full and new moon.) But don't forget the wild mulberry and black raspberry crops. Check for their purple fruits from early June below the Ohio Valley, to early July into the northern tier of states. In the South and Border States, complete setting out tobacco plants.

In the lawn, chinch bugs hatch; be sure to water heavily to counteract their damage. In your trees, look for tent caterpillars.

As the moon darkens after June 9th, hunt the bean leaf beetles that could be chewing holes in your bean leaves.

Spray for potato leafhoppers, which are hopping in the alfalfa (and the potatoes). Find the corn borers eating corn. Rose chafers and two-spotted spider mites are active in your rose bushes. Cucumber beetles are destroying cucumber and melon vines. Japanese beetles are attacking almost everything.

Take advantage of drier weather to detassel corn, to bring in the winter wheat, to complete the first cut of alfalfa and to start the second cut.

And if your animals are reinfested with worms, consider worming every 17 days to three weeks or every three lunar phases in order to eliminate the parasites.

The Moon and the Weather

Weather history indicates that cold waves will cross the Mississippi around the dates listed below. The fronts pass through the West 24 to 48 hours prior to their arrival in the Midwest; they reach the East 24 to 48 hours later.

Major storms are most likely to occur on the days between June 5 – 8, June 13 – 16, and June 24 – 28. Full moon on June 9 and new moon (combined with perigee) on June 23 are likely to bring chill and rain.

June 2

The June 2nd high-pressure ridge is typically mild, bringing a light freeze at upper elevations and in the North, but sparing almost every field and garden south of Chicago.

June 6

Thunderstorms are common between the arrival of this front and the next. The normal rise in average temperatures (this year, enhanced by full moon on the 9th) that spawns the storms across the nation also contributes to a surge in pasture growth. And if your fields and garden have been seeded late in May, this weather window often provides the moisture to initiate sprouting.

June 10

The days between this front and the next are dry more often than not, and the sun usually shines more between the 10th and 26th than during any other period in May and June.

June 15

Sun and heat usually follow the storms that precede the June 15th front, and the percentage of good field days rises. Between the 15th and the 19th, average temperatures climb their final degrees throughout the nation, reaching their summer peak near solstice.

June 23

Cooler conditions in the 70s or even the 60s are most likely to occur in the North on the 23rd and 24th, as this front arrives with today's new moon and lunar perigee, but then the afternoons usually warm to the 80s or 90s throughout the continental United States.

June 29

Summer's milder days usually come to an end as the last front of June passes through your garden, and the Corn Tassel Rains, a period of precipitation that foreshadows the advent of summer's Dog Days, often begin with July and sometimes continue through the 13th.

Almanack Phenology: When... Then

When you hear quail whistling in the woods, look for tent caterpillars in the trees.

When mulberry season peaks, then goslings leave the nest and young coyotes come after your chickens and new lambs.

When May apples have fruit the size of a cherry and honeysuckle flowers have all come down, look for cucumber beetles to reach the economic threshold on the farm.

When fireflies light up the night, chinch bugs hatch in the lawn, and powdery mildew becomes a problem in the garden phlox.

When yucca stalks are tall, young blackbirds leave their nests, and nettles have grown up to your chest. Then, Japanese beetles start to attack roses and ferns. Azalea bark scale eggs hatch, too!

When pie cherries ripen, painted turtles and box turtles lay their eggs, and giant (but harmless) stag beetles prowl the grass.

When the oakleaf hydrangea produces its first blooms, then fall webworms and mimosa webworm eggs hatch.

When day lilies bloom by the roadsides, winter wheat turns a soft, pale green.

When catalpa trees bloom, then the first raspberries redden.

When bud clusters form on the milkweeds and hosta, then oaks, Osage orange and black walnut trees have set their fruit, and cherry picking is in full swing.

When black-eyed Susans flower across the northern states, then the wheat harvest is over in the Gulf region.

When long seedpods have formed on the locust trees, then annual cicadas start to chant.

When you see the first black walnuts on the ground, then you know that this year's ducklings and goslings are nearly full grown.

A Floating Calendar of Bloom for Wildflowers, Weeds, Garden Perennials, Shrubs and Trees

June 1:   Rugosa Rose (rosa rugosa)
           Floribunda Rose   (floribunda)

	Delphinium (delphinium)
	Moth Mullein (verbascum blattaria)
June 2:	Feverfew (tanacetum parthenium)
	Heliopsis (heliopsis helianthoides)
	Quickweed (galinsoga parviflora)
June 3:	Swamp Valerian (valeriana ulginosa)
	Moneywort (lysimachia nummularia)
	Rape brassica (napus)
June 4:	Campanula (campanula rapunculus)
	Wild Garlic (allium ursinum)
	Scarlet Pimpernel (anagallis arvensis)
	Nodding Thistle (carduus nutans)
	Common "Ditch" Lily (hemerocallis fulva)
June 5:	Bindweed (convolvulus arvensis)
	Crown Vetch (securigera varia)
	Smartweed (polygonum hydropiper)
June 6:	Pickerel Plant (pontederia cordata)
	Balloon Flower (platycodon grandiflorus)
	Deptford Pink (sianthus armeria)
June 7:	Oakleaf Hydrangea (hydrangea quercifolia)
	Dogbane (apocynu cannabinum)
	Virginia Creeper (parthenocissus quinquefolia)
June 8:	Purple Coneflower (echinacea purpurea)
June 9:	Asiatic Lily (lilium asiaticum)
	Carnation (dianthus caryophylus)
	Blueweed (echium vulgare L.)
	Pokeweed (phytolacca americana)
June 10:	Early Season Hosta
	Shasta Daisy (leucanthemum maximum)
	Queen Anne's Lace (daucus carota)
	Veronica (veronica)
June 11:	Hollyhock (alcea rosea)
	Beardtongue (penstemon barbatus)
June 12:	Mallow (malva sylvestris)
	Avens (geum urbanum)
June 13:	Tall Meadow Rue (thalictrum dasycarpum)

	Great Mullein (verbascum Thapsus)
June 14:	Leatherflower (clematis pitcher)
	Common Sow Thistle (onchus oleraceus)
	Common Milkweed (asclepias syriaca)
June 15:	Large-Leafed Hostas
	Wild Petunia (ruellia humilis)
June 16:	White Sweet Clover (melilotus albus)
	Lizard's Tail (saururus cernuus L.)
June 17:	Asiatic Dayflower (commelina communis)
	Trumpet Creeper (campsis radicans)
June 18:	Japanese Iris (iris ensata)
	Narrow-Leaved Cattail (typha latifolia)
June 19:	Russian Sage (perovskia atriplicifolia)
	Black-Eyed Susan (rudbeckia hirta)
June 20:	Pale Touch-Me-Not (impatiens pallida)
June 21:	Gooseneck (lysimachia clethroides)
	Woodland Sunflower (helianthus divaricatus)
June 22:	Enchanter's Nightshade (circa Lutetian
	Figwort (scrophularia)
June 23:	Catnip (nepeta)
	Ramps (astilbe arendsii)
	Compass Plant (silphium laciniatum)
June 24:	Thimbleplant (rubus parviflorus)
	Wood Mint (blephilia ciliate)
June 25:	Bergamot (monarda didyma)
	Tall Nettle (urtica dioica)
	Horse Nettle (solanum carolinense)
June 26:	Creeping Bell Flower (campanula rapunculoides)
	Heal All (prunella)
June 27:	Limelight hydrangea(hydrangea paniculata)
	Lopseed (phryma leptostachya)
	Evening Primrose (oenothera biennis)
June 28:	Rose of Sharon (hibiscus syriacus)
	Leafcup (polymnia laevigata beadle)
June 29:	Fringed Loosestrife (lysimachi ciliate)
	Wild Lettuce (lactuca virosa)

June 30: **Butterfly Weed (asclepias tuburosa)**
St. John's Wort (hypericum
perforatum)
Teasel (dipsacus)

Peak Activity Times for Creatures

The following guide to lunar position shows when the moon is above (Best times) or below (Second-best times) the country, and, therefore, the period during which livestock, people, fish and game are typically the most active and the hungriest.

Date	Best	Second-Best
June 1:	Afternoons	Midnight to Dawn
June 2 – 9:	Evenings	Mornings
June 18 – 23:	Mornings	Evenings
June 24 – 30:	Afternoons	Midnight to Dawn

Almanack Literature
Up in a Tree
by Christine Middleton, Dayton, Ohio

I can remember now with a sort of longing when I found my own special place. I was six or seven years old, the second of nine children. Our house had three small bedrooms. I shared a room with my four sisters. We often woke up to babies crying or cupboards slamming, too many kids for parents who did not handle stress well.

Though I did escape to the pages of my Black Stallion or Nancy Drew books, the rush of kids and the moods of my parents intruded constantly. So the summer when I could finally reach the lowest bough, my maple became my hideaway.

I was the best climber of the kids and could go really high. Two branches made me a seat. The bark was smooth; the sun sparkled through the quaking leaves. I was in another world, a world with a breeze and a view. I listened to my tree by laying my ear against its bark. Did you know sound travels down through branches to the trunk? When the breeze blew the creaking from within was a language to me.

I would take my book up into the tree and spend a quiet hour. One sleepy summer afternoon: WUMP! I was on the bare dirt. I jumped up alert to who had seen me fall. I figured no more climbing if my mother had seen this! I never told.

The summer of my twelfth year with another baby coming and a bed-ridden grandparent, we finally had to move. My heart was breaking. I would leave my tree behind. The day we left I climbed higher than ever before and carved a message in the bark. In the next years, I came to find within me a place of serenity. A place I knew existed because my tree had taught me well.

July
2017

To deliver oneself up, to hand oneself over, entrust oneself completely to the silence of a wide landscape of woods and hills, or sea, or desert; to sit still while the sun comes up over the land and fills its silences with light. To pray and work in the morning and to labor and rest in the afternoon, and to sit still again in meditation in the evening when night falls upon the land and when the silence fills itself with darkness and with stars.

Thomas Merton

The Gregorian Calendar for July

S	M	T	W	T	F	S
						1
2	3	4	5	6	7	8
9	10	11	12	13	14	15
16	17	18	19	20	21	22
23	24	25	26	27	28	29
30	31					

The Butterfly and the Bird

I was sitting in the back yard enjoying the mild weather and the sun. By chance, I happened to look up into the tall locust tree at the edge of my property.

There, high on a branch, I saw a small yellow butterfly which appeared to be attacking a robin. The butterfly left its place on the branch, flew quickly at the bird, then away from it and returned to the tree. In a few seconds, it repeated the pattern. After three such assaults, the robin left, and only the insect remained, perched victorious and unmoving on the locust. The whole incident was over in less than a minute

Now, other than my personal observation, there is no evidence that butterflies can drive off robins. Like stories of frogs aggressively guarding their territories against huge pike and carp, my bird-butterfly tale lies on the fringes of natural history.

Still, the incident seems more than just an illusion created by my ignorance or by my distance from the ostensibly feuding creatures. In the quiet of middle summer I saw the meek and the fragile inherit the earth, the weak overcome the strong, and I thought that maybe if I really watched more closely, took my time, sat in the afternoon sun through all of summer,

I would witness the other beatitudes fulfilled, see the secret balance of the world revealed.

The Sweet Corn Moon and the Blackberry Moon

No matter where you live, the Sweet Corn Moon gives birth to almost all the summer and autumn crickets and katydids. And in most states, blackberries have set fruit, are still green in Wisconsin, but sweet black in the South.

June 30: The moon enters its second quarter at 7:51 a.m.
July 6: Lunar apogee (when the moon is farthest from Earth)
July 8: The Sweet Corn Moon is full at 11:07 p.m.
July 16: The moon enters its final quarter at 2:26 p.m.
July 21: Lunar perigee
July 23: The Blackberry Moon is new at 14:43 a.m.
July 30: The moon enters its second phase at 10:23 a.m.

The S.A.D. Stress Index

Seasonal affective disorder increases during the hottest days of the year. Many people who suffer from humidity and high temperatures tend to stay indoors like they do in the winter; consequently, they often experience some of the same S.A.D. symptoms they feel in December or January.

Key for Interpreting the S.A.D. Index:
Totals of 75 to 65: S.A.D. Alert: Severe Stress for those who suffer from seasonal affective disorders
64 to 50: Severe to moderate stress
49 to 35: Moderate stress
34 to 25: Light to moderate stress
24 and below: Low stress

Day	Clouds	Weather	Daylight	Totals
July 1:	0	16	0	16
July 15:	0	21	0	21
July 30:	0	18	1	19

The Sun

At 5:00 a.m. on July 3, the Earth reaches aphelion, the point at which it is about 153 million kilometers (its greatest

distance) from the Sun. Aphelion occurs almost exactly six months from perihelion, Earth's position closest to the Sun (about 148 million kilometers).

The Sun enters the late summer sign of Leo on July 23.

The Planets

♃ ♄ ♀♂

Once again moving retrograde, this time into Taurus, Venus leads Orion (as well as Sirius, the Dog Star) into the morning. Mars, still in Gemini, is not visible. Jupiter is the evening star in the far west this month. Saturn remains in Ophiuchus, traveling the southern tree line after dark above Libra and Scorpius.

The Stars

The sky of summer's aphelion reflects the parallel universe of circular time. At noon, the stars overhead are the stars of winter's perihelion midnight: Orion due south, the Pleiades overhead. On the clearest July afternoons, January's Sirius is visible in the southeast. The Big Dipper lies in the northeast, Cepheus in the northwest. Leo is rising. Pegasus is setting.

On the other hand, this week's *night* sky is the day sky of middle winter. The teapot-like star formation of Libra is prominent in the south, followed by Scorpius and its red center, Antares. Sagittarius, the Archer, follows the Scorpion in the southeast. Above the Archer, the Milky Way sweeps up toward Cassiopeia in the north.

The Shooting Stars

The nights of July 28 – 29 bring the Delta Aquarids after 12:00 a.m. in Aquarius. This shower can bring up to 20 meteors in an hour.

A Calendar of Feast Days and Holidays for Farmers, Gardeners and Homesteaders

July 4, 2017: United States (also Puerto Rico) Independence Day

Farming and Gardening with the Moon

As summer warmth continues to build, remember that water consumption requirements for livestock are between two and three times that of dry food. High protein feed that contains salt will add to an animal's need for liquid.

Watch for contamination in your animals' water, especially in the chicken house, and consider adding a water-soluble vitamin and mineral on a regular basis.

Hogs kept inside need plenty of ventilation and sometimes a good hosing down to keep them cool. Heat also increases the risk for poor air quality in the barn.

Heat can be hard on your horses, too. Be sure they have plenty of shade. And mosquitoes that spread West Nile Virus are especially dangerous to your animals; check your property for mosquito breeding areas. Efficient manure management always cuts down on flies that attack all of your livestock.

Pastures of clovers and cool-season grasses stressed by drought early in the summer can suffer more severely during stagnant July weather. Consider developing annual pastures next year that can serve as a supplement to your perennials. Some homesteaders use silage corn for grazing as pastures go dormant.

Even as the fields dry up, don't neglect to increase feed to your breeder animals, and consider a physical examination for each.

As the Dog Days intensify, keep an eye on your animals after you have transported them to county or state fairs. Be sure they have plenty of attention, feed and water, especially at full moon, perigee and new moon.

Before the moon turns full in early August, consider planting tomatoes for autumn and winter greenhouse fruit. As conditions permit, seed fall pastures and late summer greens, beans and peas. Put out cabbage, kale and collard sets. Complete the harvest of winter wheat and oats under the dark moon. Start the cutting of summer cabbage of cauliflower, too.

Late July, when the day's length has lost an average of 30 to 45 minutes from its longest span, is the typical time for does and ewes to show first signs of estrus cycling in much of the country. Check records now to estimate the cycle date for each of your animals; those dates are often similar from year to year.

Drought, heat and age contribute to declining nutritional value in grasses by this time of the summer. Variety in browse offers chances for better nourishment to your flock and herd. Some farmers have livestock graze the hay fields when the pastures give out.

The Moon and the Weather

Weather history indicates that cold waves will cross the Mississippi around the dates listed below. The fronts pass through the West 24 to 48 hours prior to their arrival in the Midwest; they reach the East 24 to 48 hours later.

Tornadoes, floods or prolonged periods of soggy pasture are most likely to occur within the following windows: July 3 – 8 and July 21 – 23. Full moon on July 8th and new moon on the 23rd are likely to coincide with storms.

The period between July 24 and August 5, on the other hand, is usually one of the most uneventful (except for Dog

Day heat) in the entire meteorological year.

July 6

The first weather system of July is associated with high heat and the Corn Tassel Rains. Thunderstorms and overcast skies precede the July 6th front, sometimes bringing hail. Even though lunar apogee takes place on the 6th, the full moon on the 7th may cause problems for travel and outdoor activities.

The wettest days of the month often come between the 2nd and the 13th. July 7, 8 and 9 are some of the worst Dog Days of the year, all three bringing at least a ten percent chance for afternoons above 100 degrees at average elevations along the 40th Parallel.

July 14

After this weather system crosses the nation, conditions are more likely to be dry and hot than wet and cool, and highs above 100 are more likely to occur at the end of July's second week than on any other days of the year.

July 21

Showers associated with this high-pressure cell often put an end to midsummer drought, and a slight break in the Dog Days is likely at lunar perigee on the 21st and new moon on the 23rd.

July 28

Although showers often precede this system, and a chilly high in the 70s sometimes follows, hot weather usually returns within a day or two.

Almanack Phenology: When... Then

When the first apple and cherry tree leaves become yellow and drift to the ground, alewives head back to sea from their estuaries along the Atlantic Ocean.

When road kills increase in summer, expect thunderstorms and intense Dog Day heat.

When mimosa webworms appear on locust trees, potato leafhoppers reach economic levels in alfalfa.

When teasel flowers along the roadsides and wood nettle blooms in the woods, then bagworms attack arborvitae, euonymus, juniper, linden, maple and fir. Root diseases stalk the soybeans, and the wheat still standing in the fields suffers from rust, powdery mildew, head scab, and glume blotch.

When elderberry flowers turn to fruit, then giant green June beetles appear in the garden and poisonous white snakeroot is budding. That's the time to dig your garlic before the heads break apart. Plant your autumn turnips right after that.

When thimbleberry, blueweed, great Indian plantain, great mullein, milkweed, black-eyed Susan, columbine, red bleeding heart, dock, daisy fleabane, large black medic bush clover, yellow and white sweet clover, cow parsnip, blue-eyed grass and Hooker's orchis flower in the Appalachians, then strawberry season is at its best in the Pacific Northwest.

When geese start getting restless, that's the time the blueberry crop will be thinning and summer apples will be about half picked.

When the first ears of corn are silking, then it's time to bring in the winter wheat and canola. That's when salmonberry bushes are in full bloom along the Columbia River and the last lilac bush flowers in the mountains of Alberta, Canada.

When milkweed pods appear on the milkweed, check your calendar and start counting the days. Those pods should burst about 80 days later at the approach of middle autumn.

When pokeweed has green berries, expect the Japanese beetles to be at their strongest in the soybeans and roses.

When morning birdsong diminishes and insect volume increases, then set out your collard, kale and cabbage sets for fall.

When sycamore trees shed their bark, they mark the center of summer.

When hemlock and parsnips turn brown and brittle in the sun, then early summer's clovers and grasses are past their prime.

When velvetleaf blooms in the fields, then expect the driest time of summer.

When wild cherries darken on the wild cherry trees, then potato leafhoppers eat your potato leaves.

When peaches ripen in the Midwest, then strawberries are coming in throughout Ontario, and peonies are still flowering on homesteads along the northern rim of the Great Lakes.

When wild grapes ripen, then begin the dry onion harvest.

When the green fruit of the osage orange is big and fat enough to come down in thunderstorm winds, then look for swallows to be congregating on the high wires, resting on their way south.

When Joe Pye weed sends out its purple flowers in the wetlands, then farmers are preparing for August seeding of alfalfa.

When late crickets start to chant, look for a few Judas maples to produce red and orange foliage, and then finish the cutting of winter grains.

When you see seedpods fully formed

on the trumpet creepers and green berries on the poison ivy, and when white vervain blossoms reach the end of their spikes, then listen for katydids to begin shouting "katy-did" after dark.

When ragweed comes into bloom, then a few cottonwoods are turning pale with age, and patches of yellow appear on the weaker ash tees.

When black walnut leaves start to fall, then middle summer is coming to an end, and meadowlarks have begun their southward migration, and pokeweed berries darken.

A Floating Calendar of Bloom for Wildflowers, Weeds, Garden Perennials, Shrubs and Trees

July 1:	Bouncing Bets (saponaria officinalis)
	Wood Nettle (laportea canadensis)
July 2:	Mid-Season Garden Phlox (phlox paniculata)
	Tall Bell Flower (campanula americana)
July 3:	Oriental Lilies
	Ginseng (panax)
July 4:	Liatris (liatris spicata)
	Grey-Headed Coneflower (ratibida pinnata)
July 5:	Obedient Plant (physostegia virginiana)
July 6:	White Vervain (verbena urticifolia)
July 7:	Oxeye (chrysanthemum \ leucanthemum)
	Horseweed (conyza canadensis)
July 9:	Germander (teucrium canadense)

	Small-Flowered Agrimony (agrimonia parviflora)
July 10:	Showy Coneflower (rudbeckia alpicola)
July 11:	Skullcap (scutellaria lateriflora)
July 12:	Fogfruit (phyla nodiflora)
	Great Indian Plantain (arnoglossum reniforme)
July 14:	Wingstem (verbesina alternifolia)
	Blue Vervain (verbena hastate)
July 16:	Butterfly Bush (buddleja davidii)
July 17:	Tick Trefoil (desmodium canadense)
	Thin-Leaved Coneflower (rudbeckia triloba)
July 18:	Velvet Leaf (abutilon theophrasti)
	Bull Thistle (cirsium vulgare)
July 19:	Water Hemlock (cicuta maculate)
	Early Goldenrod (solidago)
July 20:	Resurrection Lily (lycoris squamigera)
July 21:	Burdock (arctium lappa)
July 22:	Ironweed (vernonia gigantean)
	Monkey Flower (mimulus guttatus)
	Arrowhead (sagittaria latifolia)
July 23:	Stonecrop Autumn Joy Sedum (sedum)
	Joe Pye Weed (eutrochium purpureum)
July 23:	Turk's Cap Lily (lilium superbium)
	Jimson Weed (datura stramonium)
July 24:	Field Thistle (cirisium arvense)
	Common Ragweed (ambrosia artemisiifolia)
July 25:	Tall Coneflower (rudbeckia laciniata)
	Narrow-Leaved Mountain Mint pycnanthemum tenuifolium)
July 27:	Biennial Gaura (gaura biennis)
July 28:	White Snakeroot (ageratina altissima)
July 29:	Clearweed (pilea pumila)
July 30:	Jumpseed (persicaria virginiana)
July 31:	Boneset (eupatorium perfoliatum)
	Pigweed (amaranthus palmeri)

Peak Activity Times for Creatures

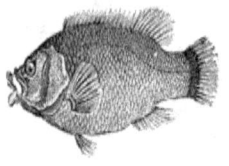

The following guide to lunar position shows when the moon is above (Best times) or below (Second-best times) the country, and, therefore, the period during which livestock, people, fish and game are typically the most active and the hungriest.

Date	Best	Second-Best
July 1 – 7:	Evenings	Mornings
July 8 – 15:	Midnight to Dawn	Afternoons
July 16 – 22:	Mornings	Evenings
July 23 – 31:	Afternoons	Midnight to Dawn

Almanack Literature
Naming the Cows
by Larry Rader, Shiloh, Ohio

During my teaching career in public high schools, a top priority for me was learning the names of 140 – 150 boys and girls during the first week of classes. I had a lot of practice with learning names during the summer months and on weekends because I helped a dairy farmer with chores.

Occasionally, he had me help him in

the milking parlor, and as time went on, I spent more and more time milking the cows. To identify each cow, the dairlyman did not use the conventional chain and tag; he had given each a name!

At first, learning the names of about 180 Holstein cows (they all looked alike: black and white and all female) seemed impossible to me. But slowly, I learned that each cow was not only different physically but also in behavior.

There was a definite pecking order. Usually the first 50 or so cows and the last 50 or so cows were consistently entering in a certain order; if a cow was sick or injured, she would be lagging toward the end.

Little by little I also learned the names of all the cows, and the dairyman eventually trusted me enough to go on rare vacations, and once to see the Buckeyes play in the Rose Bowl.

Here are the names of the cows: Abby, Alice, Allison, Amanda, Amy....

(Mr. Rader remembered and included ALL the names (a total of 191) from Abby all the way to Zelma in his letter to Poor Will!)

AUGUST
2017

The trails I made led outward into the hills and swamps, but they led inward also. And from the study of things underfoot, and from reading and thinking, came a kind of exploration of myself and the land. In time the two became one in my mind.

John Haines

The Gregorian Calendar for August

S	M	T	W	T	F	S
		1	2	3	4	5
6	7	8	9	10	11	12
13	14	15	16	17	18	19
20	21	22	23	24	25	26
27	28	29	30	31		

Nostalgia

Come, let us climb the Lord's mountain....
Isaiah 2:3

This morning, I was wandering in the woods when I came across a small pool surrounded by bare saplings, a pond in a glade, reminiscent of the flooded field I played in as a boy one August. And then from the memory of that pond I recalled so many beaches and dreams.

In these moods of mine, nothing is ever what it appears to be; one thing becomes the sign of another. Like children playing the game of telephone, I dialogue with myself until my thoughts come full circle, transformed into something completely different from the image that began the conversation.

Later in the day, I was driving south through the August fog. I settled back in the truck and watched the countryside, looked out at the farm ponds, gray and still. Like the morning's perfect glade, the ponds became transformed to something else, an experience in the phosphorescent tropical sea in 1960. An entire tapestry of my life passed through my brain, guided only by a highway landscape that transcended the modernity and speed of the vehicle in which I was driving, and that tied me to the words and acts I had known and lost and regained.

Once, before freeways, I drove east through the Great Smoky Mountains in the rain and the dark, winding through the night, holding my breath at each curve, until I finally emerged onto the broad flatlands of South Carolina. Ahead of me lay sunrise and the coastal plain, the treacherous hills gone, the way made straight. Everything seemed now within my grasp.

Then that feeling of freedom and possibility led to something else: vague promises tied to the romance of the receding road, the prospect of a promised land, a far castle like a mountain of the Lord.

Tonight, the recollections around me here are subtle dendrites extending from within and from without, pulling me deeper into their tangles. The pond and the glade and the highway are sanctuaries for a moment, perfect and satisfying, but then they always take me somewhere else. The end is the passage.

The Blackberry Moon and the Cricket and Katydid Moon

Dark blackberries usher in the season of late summer. When they are ripe enough to pick, then all the crickets and katydids sing through the nights, and the first bird migrations are underway.

August 2: Lunar apogee (when the moon is farthest from Earth)

August 7: The moon is full at 1:11 p.m.

August 14: The moon enters its final quarter at 8:15 p.m.

August 18: Lunar perigee (when the moon is closest to Earth)

August 21: The Cricket and Katydid Moon is new at 1:30 p.m.

August 29: The moon enters its second phase at 3:13 a.m.

The S.A.D. Stress Index

In late summer, seasonal affective disorder typically depends more on heat and humidity than on the day's length or cloud cover. The likelihood of cooler weather toward the end of the month contributes to a lightening of summer cabin fever.

Key for Interpreting the S.A.D. Index:
Totals of 75 to 65: Severe Stress
64 to 50: Severe to moderate stress
49 to 35: Moderate stress
34 to 25: Light to moderate stress
24 and below: Low Stress

Day	Clouds	Weather	Daylight	Totals
August 1:	0	18	3	21
August 15:	0	16	5	21
August 30	0	11	9	18

The Sun

This month, the sun moves halfway between summer solstice and autumn equinox, entering Virgo and reaching Cross-Quarter Day on August 23.

A total eclipse of the Sun occurs on August 21, visible in its entirety in an area from Oregon through the center of the United States. The eclipse will begin in the middle of the morning and will last until the middle of the afternoon.

The Planets

Moving retrograde above Orion into Gemini, Venus holds on to its position as the morning star. Mars, in Cancer, is still hidden from view. Jupiter remains in Virgo, low on the western skyline at dusk. Saturn lies below Hercules at sundown, disappears into the west after midnight.

The Stars
August is the month of the Milky Way in the eastern early night sky.

Cygnus the swan can be found there, its formation a giant cross. Below it is Aquila, spreading from its keystone, Altair, like a great eagle. Almost directly overhead, Vega of the constellation Lyra is the brightest star in the heavens. Hercules stands beside it. June's Corona Borealis and the huge Arcturus have moved to the west.

The Shooting Stars

The Perseid meteors peak August 11 through 13 in the east an hour or so after midnight below the Milky Way in Perseus. This shower can produce up to 60 meteors in an hour. If you look too far to the east, you will see Orion emerging out of the trees. If you look too far west, you will see the Great Square.

Calendar of Feast Days and Holidays for Farmers, Gardeners and Homesteaders

August 7: Jamaican Independence Day

August 10: Ecuadorian Independence Day

Farming and Gardening with the Moon

Sodding and seeding of the lawn is often done throughout August (especially around the time that the moon turns new) before the cooler days of fall. Test soil in your fall and winter garden as well as in the fields where you intend to sow wheat, rye, alfalfa, canola, clover and timothy.

Cut corn for silage after completing the second and third cuts of hay. Dig potatoes and pick commercial tomato plants clean. Complete harvest of everbearing strawberries, plums, pears, watermelons, blackberries and peaches in the South; then move north to start all over.

The breeding season opens for your goats and sheep. Consider supplements for the rams and bucks: carrots, oats, bran, iodized salt and good greens are popular additions to feed.

As temperatures gradually move toward fall, check the average killing frost date in your area, then subtract 30 days for light frost, and 30 more days for the chance of a slight frost (enough to hurt delicate market crops like basil). Before a freeze (most likely after full and new moons), gather up the squash and pumpkins if their stems are dry; store in a cool, dry location.

When frost hurts root crops, don't feed them to your pregnant animals. The frost may change the composition of the roots, contributing to abortions.

The Moon and the Weather

Weather history suggests that cold waves will cross the Mississippi around the dates listed below. The fronts pass through the West 24 to 48 hours prior to their arrival in the Midwest; they reach the East 24 to 48 hours later.

Tornadoes, floods or prolonged periods of soggy pasture are most likely to occur within the following windows: August 7 – 13, and August 27 – 30. Frost is most likely, of course, as summer ends, but the last cold front of the month often burns tender plants all along the northern border with Canada and at higher elevations. Full moon on August 7, perigee on the 18th, and new moon on the 21st are likely to strengthen fronts due near those dates.

August 4

After this weather system moves across the land, the likelihood for highs in the 90s begins a steady decline all along the 40th Parallel, and the possibility for a high only in the 60s increases across the northern tier of states. Full moon on the 7th is likely to increase the chances for precipitation between this front and the August 10th system.

August 10

The August 10th cool front can bring frost to the higher elevations in the West and often causes thunderstorms throughout the Plains and the South. Full moon on the 7th is likely to increase the likelihood of dangerous weather. After passage of high pressure, average temperatures in most of the country drop one to two degrees per week until September 10th, after which point they decline at least one degree every three days into January.

August 17

As late summer deepens, the chances for snow and frost increase at higher elevations, and the August 17th front begins the transition from summer stability to autumn unpredictability in the North. Sudden cold snaps and strong autumnal winds can now chill your livestock still grazing in the mountains, and perigee on the 18th, combined with new moon on the 21st, may increase the chances for cold. Humidity, however, builds up at lower elevations and in the central and southern regions, and heat in the 80s and 90s is still the rule.

August 24

Now the likelihood of severe heat in the nation's midsection is only half of what it was at the beginning of August, and chances for light frost increase along the Canadian border. Across the South, however, this front brings little change.

August 29

Higher elevations and the northernmost states can expect the threat of a freeze or flurries with this weather system.

Almanack Phenology: When...Then

When honeysuckle berries ripen, and hickory nuts and black walnuts drop into the undergrowth, then dig your potatoes.

When green acorns fall to the sweet rocket growing back for next year's flowers, then black walnut trees will have lost about a third of their leaves and hummingbirds, wood ducks, Baltimore orioles and purple martins start to move south.

When the violet Joe Pye weed flowers become gray like the thistledown, then peaches, processing tomatoes and peppers are almost all picked, and the fruit of the bittersweet ripens orange.

When watermelons are ripe and firefly season comes to a close, then cut the last of your oats and put in your fall peas.

When spiders start to increase their building of webs in the woodlot, then yellow jacket season begins in the windfall apples and plums, and morning fogs increase in the lowlands.

When the first field corn is mature, then divide and transplant the lily-of-the-valley.

When cardinals stop singing before dawn, watch the soybean leaves yellowing in the fields and get ready to cut corn for silage.

When velvet leaf goes to seed in Midwestern fields, then frost time approaches for pastures in the Rocky Mountains.

When you see long flocks of blackbirds moving across the sky, then it's time for plums to be the sweetest of the year.

After you pick the last of the elderberries, then scout the fields for late-season pests: second-brood corn borers, second-generation bean leaf beetles and rootworm beetles.

When the first wild grape is sweet, then prepare the soil for the planting of winter grains.

When all the summer apples have been picked, then look for the first puffball mushroom of the year to swell in the cool, damp nights.

When you see more than one Judas maple tree in the woodlot, then hickory nutting season gets underway.

When red leaves appear on the Virginia creeper in Kentucky, then snow threatens gardens in central Canada.

When the last garden phlox dies back, then ragweed time winds down and the year's final tier of wildflowers is budding: beggarticks, bur marigolds, asters, zigzag goldenrod.

When the midseason hostas and the lilies are gone, summer stabilizes again, solid in the gold and purple coneflowers, the tall wingstem and ironweed, the rich opening of the ragweed, the green budding stalks of the goldenrod poised, their full season still ahead, reassuring, promising the long-lived asters soon.

When dogbane pods turn reddish brown in the fields, then wood nettle has gone to seed under the high canopy.

When elm trees start to turn, then

watch for mallards flying south. Whip-poor-wills, cedar waxwings and catbirds follow.

When greenbrier berries are black, then prickly mallow blooms along the fencerows and almost all the oats crop has been cut.

When the last summer apples have been picked, then the wood thrush migrates south across the Ohio River.

When arrowhead blooms in the waterways, then pale Asian lady beetles beginlate migration.

A Floating Calendar of Bloom for Wildflowers, Weeds, Garden Perennials, Shrubs and Trees

August 1: Mad-Dog Skullcap (scutellaria lateriflora)
Giant Yellow Hyssop (agastache nepetoides)
August 2: Prickly Mallow (sida spinosa)
Great Ragweed (ambrosia trifida)
August 3: Milk Purslane (euphorbia maculate)
August 4: Willow Herb (epilobium)
August 5: Japanese Knotweed (fallopian japonica)
August 7: Love Vine (cassytha filiformis)
August 8: False Boneset (brickellia eupatoriodes or Kuhnia eupatoriodes)
August 9: Bur Cucumber (cucumis anguria)
August 10: Three-Seeded Mercury (acalypha rhomboidea)
August 11: Water Horehound (lycopus americanus)
August 12: Tall Goldenrod (solidago)
August 14: Great Blue Lobelia (lobelia siphilitica)

August 16:   Rose Pink (glandularia canadensis)
August 23:   Hog Peanut (amphicarpaea bracteata)
August 24:   Jerusalem Artichoke (heliantus
                    tuberosus)
August 29:   Beggarticks (bidens pilosa or frondosa)
August 30:   Bur Marigold (bidens tripartite)
August 31:   Heath Aster (symphyotrichum
                    ericoides)

Peak Activity Times for Creatures

The following guide to lunar position shows when the moon is above (Best times) or below (Second-best times) the country, and, therefore, the period during which livestock, people, fish and game are typically the most active and the hungriest.

Date	Best	Second-Best
August 1 – 6:	Evenings	Mornings
August 7 – 13:	Midnight to Dawn	Afternoons
August 14 – 20:	Mornings	Evenings
August 21 – 28:	Afternoons	Midnight to Dawn
August 29 – 31:	Evenings	Mornings

Almanack Literature

The Story of the Rambunctious Rooster
by Myrna Glass, Saint Marys, Ohio

My Aunt Frances was blind. She spent her time visiting with her brothers and sisters. My brothers and I, as well as all of our cousins, looked forward to her visits because she was so much fun.

She had a repertoire of stories that you wouldn't believe. If a child wanted a "bear story," Aunt Frances came up with one. When we were teens, we regaled her with stories of our dating and "puppy love" stories that we wouldn't have thought of telling our parents!

We had no indoor plumbing at that time, only "six rooms and a path," and I had the dubious honor of escorting Aunt Frances to the outhouse.

One summer, we had a rambunctious rooster. When I went to the outhouse alone, I would check his location, and then make a run for it to keep him from pecking my bare legs.

When I was escorting Aunt Frances, I'd keep an eye out for him and give him a kick to discourage him. That tough old bird was not discouraged. He kept on trying.

Then, once on our way through the chicken yard, I saw him coming. I let go of Auntie and said, "Just a minute!" Then I really gave him a kick that sent him flying.

Auntie said, "What was that noise?"

I answered, "It was that old rooster. I gave him such a kick that he'll never bother us again."

He really didn't. I'd sent him to rooster heaven. Tough old bird that he was, he made a wonderful Sunday dinner, along with some of Mom's homemade noodles. That was the glorious end of the rambunctious rooster!

SEPTEMBER 2017

*Out of the west the wind comes over,
over the yellow goldenrod,
over the drying rattle-box pod,
comes heady with corn and apple smell
now.*

August Derleth

The Gregorian Calendar for September

S	M	T	W	T	F	S
					1	2
3	4	5	6	7	8	9
10	11	12	13	14	15	16
17	18	19	20	21	22	23
24	25	26	27	28	29	30

The Monks of Ellis Pond

One autumn Sunday morning, I took part in a walking meditation at a local park, Glen Helen. After instructions about how to do this practice, the participants set out in a line to follow the leader. We walked very slowly and silently.

Hikers and lovers and families with

children moved by us quickly. I had joked before the walk how we all should wear long robes so that people might know that we were meditating, but, in fact, I didn't need a robe to feel separated from the non-meditators. I cocooned inside the file of walkers.

Two days later, I took my ancient border collie, Bella, for a short outing to Ellis Pond, a small lake a mile from my house. The wind was quiet and the water smooth at the approach of the remnant of Hurricane Patricia. The ash trees and sugar maples were bare, one red oak was chocolate brown and caramel gold, the sycamores three-fourths empty. On the far shore, the cypress foliage was rusting.

When I was about to leave, I looked over toward the arboretum's grove of oaks to see if they were shedding. That was when I saw the geese. Out of a cornfield they emerged, two or three abreast, solemnly waddling at about the speed of walking meditators, their plumage like monkish habits, gray and white (except for the one white goose that always stays with that flock), forming a long, formal anserine procession.

The file passed by the brush and shallows at the northwest end of the pond and plodded toward me where the bank was not so high. When the leader reached the edge, it remained there for a moment as though taking stock of the slope of the land. The others stopped behind him, not breaking ranks. When their guru slid gracefully into the water, each meditator in turn pondered, decided, followed, at least five dozen of them I counted, and they swam out single file onto the still pond.

These were, I assumed, the same seemingly secular geese that fed and mated and raised their young in the field across from the park, the one white tagalong goose pretty much clinching my guess.

And I know that these birds fly back and forth sometimes, and gather in the pond sometimes, and have loud conversations and quarrels. But I didn't know their cenobitic fellowship was also marginally Trappist and that their occasional practices included moving contemplation, their liturgy as disciplined as that of dharmic seekers in the Glen.

The Cricket and Katydid Moon and the Corn Harvest Moon

Although harvest of fruits and vegetables has been taking place all summer, the harvest of field corn is one of the major turning points in the farm year. Now the entire northern half of the United States and Canada brings in corn for silage and grain.

September 6: The Cricket and Katydid Moon is full at 2:03 a.m.
September 13: The moon enters its final quarter at 1:25 a.m. and lunar perigee (when the moon is closest to Earth)
September 20: The Corn Harvest Moon is new at 12:30 a.m.
September 27: The moon enters its second quarter at 8:54 p.m. and reaches apogee (when it is farthest from Earth).

The S.A.D. Stress Index

September's relatively pleasant temperatures and clear skies keep seasonal affective disorder at bay throughout most of the month. In addition, hormonal energy may increase at this time of year, creating an "autumn surge" that combats S.A.D.

Totals of 75 to 65: S.A.D. Alert: Severe Stress for those who suffer from seasonal affective disorders
64 to 50: Severe to moderate stress
49 to 35: Moderate stress
34 to 25: Light to moderate stress
24 and below: Low stress

Day	Clouds	Weather	Daylight	Totals
September 1:	0	8	9	19
September 15:	2	9	10	21
September 30:	4	12	13	29

The Sun

Autumn equinox occurs (and the Sun enters its middle autumn sign of Libra) at 3:02 p.m. on September 22. Within several days of that moment, the night is about 12 hours long almost everywhere in the continental United States.

The Planets

Falling back into Leo, Venus comes up due east before dawn, accompanied by her new consort, Mars. Jupiter lingers in Virgo deep in the far west just after sundown. Saturn, following Jupiter with Ophiuchus, lies in the west after sunset.

The Stars

By sunrise, Orion has shifted to the center of the heavens. January's Leo and its brightest star, Regulus, have come up in the east, and the Great Square is following Hercules into the Ocean.

Calendar of Feast Days and Holidays for Farmers, Gardeners and Homesteaders

September 1 – 2, 2017: Eid Al-Adha: (Festival of Sacrifice) Lambs and kids in the range of 55 to 80 pounds are favored for this market.

September 4, 2017: Labor Day

September 20 – 22, 2017: Rosh Hashanah: Jewish New Year and first High Holiday.

September 21 – 29, 2017: Navaratri /Navadurgara: This Hindu feast honors the goddess Durga. Female animals are typically not used for this celebration.

September 21 – October 19, 2017: Al Hijira: Islamic New Year will continue for

29 days. No religious significance, but like many New Year celebrations, it is a cultural event. A rise in halal sales could be expected during this period.

September 30 – October 1, 2017: Ashura: This date commemorates the martyrdom of Muhammad's grandson, Hussein. It also celebrates Noah's survival from the Great Flood.

Farming and Gardening with the Moon

Watch for the pasture to shift towards its autumn composition as the number of plants available for browse starts to diminish and the rate of growth begins to slow.

As the moon wanes, (after the 6th) put in scilla, snowdrops, tulips, daffodils, and crocuses. Peonies and other perennials may be fertilized to encourage improved flowering.

Along with the chillier days comes a rapid decline in the number of wildflowers in bloom and a slowing of pasture growth. If you are running out of pasture, plan for next year's fields: late producers like oats and summer-seeded brassicas could extend your pasture season considerably.

Prepare cold frames in northern states. When the corn harvest is completed, be sure to vaccinate for entero-toxemia the lambs and kids you let run in the cornfields.

Since the equinox is a pivot point for the day's length to fall below 12 hours, you may want to turn on a low-wattage light bulb in the chicken house in order to counter the effects of the shortening days on egg production.

Rheumatic ailments in livestock and humans often become more common as autumn chill sinks in and lunar influence grows stronger at new and full moon times.

The Moon and the Weather

Weather history indicates that cold waves will cross the Mississippi around the dates listed below.

Tornadoes, hail, floods or prolonged

periods of soggy pasture are most likely to occur in connection with tropical storms, especially near full moon (September 6th), lunar perigee (September 13th) and new moon (September 20th).

September 2

This front belongs to summer more than it does to autumn, offering few major changes and providing a period of relative meteorological calm after its passage. Northern gardeners, however, can expect light frost after this weather system moves east, and snow in the mountains of the West becomes more likely with each passing front.

September 8

The September 8th weather system usually ushers in the season of early fall, and full moon on the 6th is very likely to strengthen this front.

September 12

This front brings only a slight chance for frost in most of the nation; it does, however, arrive at the time during which the average amount of daily sunshine begins to fall more rapidly, accelerating your livestock's sensitivity to the shortening days. In addition, lunar perigee on the 13th will make this front stronger.

September 15
This weather system is accompanied by increased chances for much cooler afternoon high temperatures (highs sometimes just in the 50s in the North).

September 20
The equinox front often brings a likelihood of frost as it departs east, and today's new moon increases the probability of cold. At average elevations along the 40th Parallel, chances for a light freeze are now about 30 percent per night.

September 24
The September 24th weather system brings some relief from lingering Dog Days in the South; it also extends frost season down into the Mid-Atlantic states, chances for damaging temperatures doubling over the chances before the equinox front.

September 29
The chances for light frost with this front are reduced by lunar apogee on the 27th, but average temperatures now start to fall at the rate of about four degrees per week throughout the nation.

Almanack Phenology: When... Then

When asters bloom in the waysides and bur marigolds flower in the swamps, then cut corn for silage.

When zigzag goldenrod blossoms in the woods, then the rose of Sharon shrubs drop most of their flowers and the great decline of summer wildflowers begins in the fields.

When you see fallen leaves starting to accumulate in the backwaters and farm ponds, then the grapes on your grape arbor should be getting ripe, and half of your tomatoes and potatoes should be harvested.

When the first black walnut trees are almost bare, then the third cut of alfalfa is typically complete and farmers are preparing the soil for planting canola, grasses and small grains.

When bright patches of scarlet sumac and Virginia creeper mark the fencerows, and streaks of gold have appeared on the silver olive bushes, then kingbirds, finches, ruddy ducks, herring gulls and yellow-bellied sapsuckers move south. The last young grackles and hummingbirds leave their nests. Cedar waxwings fly away. Bobolinks and woodcocks follow.

When katydids refuse to chant and crickets songs are slow, then be ready to cover your tender flowers and vegetables:

frost could be on the way that night.

When squirrels scatter buckeye hulls along the trails and locust pods fall beside them, then the first soybeans are ready to harvest.

When you see farmers planting wheat in northern fields, know that throughout the South, cotton growers are defoliating their cotton plants, a process that increases fiber quality.

When cobwebs are all over in the woods, that's the time to pick the fall apples.

When you see red berries on the silver olives, orange berries on the American mountain ash, and purple berries on the pokeweed, then violet autumn crocuses blossom in town.

When you see migrating toads in the garden on the cooler evenings, then ragweed season is coming to a close.

When the autumn leafturn starts along the 40th parallel, the deciduous trees are bare in northern Canada. In New England and in the Rocky Mountains, foliage colors are approaching their best.

When the huge pink mallows of the wetlands have died back, then the juniper tip midge appears on junipers, and gall adelgids attack the spruce threes.

When milkweed pods open, then late hosta bloom comes to a close in town. In the woods, middle spring's sedum is growing stronger.

When most of the black walnuts have fallen and wood nettle seeds are black and brittle, then begin your autumn bulb planting and transplanting of perennials in the garden.

When the day's length falls below 12 hours, then the sugar beet, pear, cabbage and cauliflower harvests commence in the Great Lakes region.

In Wisconsin, Massachusetts, New Jersey, Oregon and Washington State, the cranberry harvest begins as blue crabs become more plentiful along the Atlantic.

When goldenrod flowers are tufted and gray, then daddy longlegs disappear from the undergrowth.

A Floating Calendar of Bloom for Wildflowers, Weeds, Garden Perennials, Shrubs and Trees

September 1: New England Aster (symphyotrichum novae-angliae)
September 8: Zigzag Goldenrod (solidago flexicaulis)
September 9: Small White Aster (symphyotrichum ericoides)
Heart-Leafed Aster (symphyotrichum cordifolium)
September 10: Panicled Aster (symphyotrichum lanceolatum

Peak Activity Times for Creatures

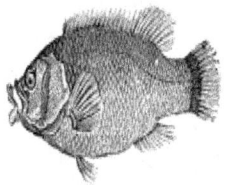

The following guide to lunar position shows when the moon is above (Best times) or below (Second-best times) the country, and, therefore, the period during which livestock, people, fish and game are typically the most active and the hungriest.

Date	Best	Second-Best
September 1 – 5:	Evenings	Mornings
September 6 – 12:	Midnight to Dawn	Afternoons
September 13 – 19:	Mornings	Evenings
September 20 – 26:	Afternoons	Midnight to Dawn
September 27 – 30:	Evenings	Mornings

Almanack Literature
Memories of a Century Past:
One Little Farmgirl's Lessons
of Thrift and Joy
by Elizabeth Doren, Oswegatchie, New York

The last time I drove by that old north country farm where I grew up nearly a century ago, I noted many changes: a swimming pool in the front yard, a new very fancy porch, and a wide driveway with several power-driven vehicles in it, leading out to the barn three times the size it used to be.

But my mind's eyes are blind to the things as they are today, and still see the old porch with its wildflower garden. Yes, and even the orchard reaching far up to the old family cemetery where our great grandparents were buried, their son who died at nineteen, and another son who died at the age of ten, the one my father spoke of fondly as Johnnie. That little cemetery looms large in my mind's eye, but something else seems larger: that chord struck down through the ages in my own family's philosophy.

When I was a child life was simpler. If you needed money, you earned it. No allowance, no handouts, but plenty of jobs. Some were routine, like doing dishes, making your bed, cleaning your room, feeding the chickens, gathering the eggs, pulling weeds in the garden, and a dozen others that you were given by virtue of being a member of the family.

But in addition to these routine chores there were special nuggets of opportunity, where you worked for real money, and seemingly the sky was the limit of what you might make.

Back in those days a junk man came around every few months and paid real money for rusty nails and scrap metal of all sorts. Getting rid of rusty nails was a worthy end on a farm powered by horses. I watched the procedure of taking care of a horse's foot injured by stepping on a nail, in the days before penicillin. My father made a solution of disinfectants and treated the foot twice a day for weeks, or so it seemed to me. He picked up the horse's foot, turned it bottom side up, cleaned it and bathed it with the pink strong-smelling disinfectant.

It worked, and the horse was soon back in harness, and we were paid a penny a pound by the junk man for all the rusty nails we collected around the farm. Some years later we heard that the junk man's son had gone to law school. Our rusty nails traveled far!

Other jobs worth real money included pulling daisies, lovely to look at, but a bane to the farmer intent on raising hay. These we collected in a gunny sack and sold to our father for a penny a pound. Shame on the greedy child who neglected to shake out the heavy clods of earth that clung to the roots!

One time I planted sweet corn, several long rows of it. I weeded and hoed it until finally the harvest was ready. It was no chore to pick the plump full ears, and no problem to sell them to a hotel in town. I happily drove a horse and buggy the ten miles to market. At ten cents a dozen I made a real killing on that venture, and my father never charged me anything for the use of the land, or the manure I carefully shoveled out to fertilize it. If you think ten cents a dozen low for sweet corn, consider the difference in the price of maple syrup. High class first run was two dollars a gallon back then. Now you're lucky to find it for thirty-six dollars, and it's thinner than it used to be.

But the real killing we made in the market was when our folks "went into strawberries," acres of them, it seemed to me. Picking strawberries falls into the category of "stoop labor," but small children don't have to stoop far to gather in the luscious fruit, and if now and then one pops into a hungry mouth the labor doesn't seem so bad. It should be easy to pick a crateful or two in the early hours before the sun becomes too hot.

Around this time our enterprising mother had persuaded our equally enterprising father to let her acquire a little herd of Shetland ponies. She had located them in Canada. There was a stallion and two mares and three colts, the prettiest little ponies you ever saw. The stallion and two mares had originally come from the Shetland Islands and they whinnied with a real burr. Along with the ponies was a neat little carriage and two full sets of harness. This was just the outfit for peddling berries.

Imagine! A team of ponies drives up to your door with a load of fresh-picked strawberries. It didn't take long for us to unload the day's picking at ten cents a quart!

Strawberry season was a busy time for us, picking, peddling, canning, shortcake making. In fact the whole farm kept us all deeply occupied in those early growing-up years, now so long ago and far away.

OCTOBER 2017

Now, too, the first of October, or later, the elms are at the height of their autumnal beauty, great brownish-yellow masses, warm from their September oven, hanging over the highway. Their leaves are perfectly ripe. I wonder if there is any answering ripeness in the lives of the men who live beneath them.

Henry David Thoreau, *Excursions*

The Gregorian Calendar for October

S	M	T	W	T	F	S
1	2	3	4	5	6	7
8	9	10	11	12	13	14
15	16	17	18	19	20	21
22	23	24	25	26	27	28
29	30	31				

Self-Deception

It is often late September when I make my trip into Kentucky to meditate for a few days at Gethsemani monastery.

I rarely see the monastery at any other time of year, and my trip takes me out of the circular context of the world of the village in which I normally live. When I arrive for my retreat, the same flowers are always in bloom, the same trees are turning, the same birds singing. Nothing has changed since the last time I came. Time has been held still by place.

At home, I find no such stability. Every day, the markers of the year change just a little. The anchor is pulled up with each sunrise. Nothing stays the same. But at Gethsemani, like a childhood memory of home or a distant summer of love, like an old photograph revisited, or a repeating dream, the season remains frozen to its context.

Before dawn, the sky spreads so deep above me, Orion always at the same stage of his ascent in the east, the Pleiades always overhead. Away from city lights, the sky is so dark and clear that I can always see the legs of Taurus, not just his red eye like here at home, and the Milky Way is almost as bright as a moon.

Inside the chapel, the sun falls through the tall stained glass windows at the same angle at Vespers as it did last year and the year before and the year before. The solar clock has stopped here, has not passed through winter or spring or summer.

I too am the same year after year, always looking for the same answers, never coming full circle, always staying suspended in autumn, never finished. Maybe that is all well and good. I will die, after all, in the world of circles, within the whole turn of some near or distant year. But in the few hours of retreat, I step outside the loop, hide from the inevitable, stand still in self-deception.

The Corn Harvest Moon and the Apple Cider Moon

The last apple crop of the year is picked throughout the autumn, and cider is just one of its many products. Like maple syrup time that marks the transition from winter to spring, cider time leads to leaf turn and leaf fall and then to winter.

October 5: The moon is full 1:40 p.m.
October 9: Lunar perigee (when the moon is closest to Earth)
October 12: The moon enters its second quarter at 7:25 a.m.
October 19: The Apple Cider Moon is new at 2:12 p.m.

October 24: Lunar apogee (the moon's position farthest from Earth)
October 27: The moon enters its second quarter at 5:23 p.m.

The S.A.D. Stress Index

Seasonal affective disorder becomes more frequent in October as the length of the night increases and chances for mild weather decrease. Although cloud cover is ordinarily not a major factor in S.A.D. during middle autumn, the odds for completely overcast conditions rise steadily.

Key for Interpreting the S.A.D. Index:
Totals of 75 to 65: S.A.D. Alert: Severe Stress for those who suffer from seasonal affective disorders
64 to 50: Severe to moderate stress
49 to 35: Moderate stress
34 to 25: Light to moderate stress
24 and below: Low stress

Day	Clouds	Weather	Daylight	Totals
October 1:	5	12	14	31
October 15:	7	15	17	39
October 31:	10	16	20	46

The Sun

October 24 is Cross Quarter Day, the halfway mark between autumn equinox and winter solstice. The Sun enters the late autumn constellation of Scorpio at the same time. Within a little more than a month of equinox, the Sun has sped half the distance to winter. If it continued to move lower in the sky at that rate for another month, solstice would occur near Thanksgiving. As December approaches, however, the expansion of the night gradually slows, finally stopping abruptly before Christmas.

The Planets

♃ ♄ ♂ ♀

Now Venus is in Virgo, retaining its position as the morning star, continuing to be shadowed by Mars (the two planets in conjunction on October 5). Jupiter blends with the sunset, disappearing from view by October 15. Saturn is still visible along the western horizon at dusk.

The Stars

The Pleiades, and the Hyades of Taurus lie on the eastern horizon well after dark, announcing middle autumn in the Northern Hemisphere. Nonetheless, summer's Milky Way is still almost directly overhead, and June's Corona Borealis has still not set by ten o'clock. Orion has not yet vanquished Hercules. Cygnus, the swan is still high above you in the west, along with August's Aquila and Lyra.

The Shooting Stars

The Draconid meteors fall (at the rate of about ten per hour) in the vicinity of the North Star after midnight on the 7th. The gibbous moon will make viewing difficult.

The Orionid meteors, children of Halley's Comet, appear in Orion during the early morning hours of October 21 and 22 at the rate of 15 to 30 per hour. The dark moon will favor viewing them.

Calendar of Feast Days and Holidays for Farmers, Gardeners and Homesteaders

October 4 – 5, 2017: Harvest Moon Festival: Chuseok: Often observed by Korean Americans and others of Asian descent.

Farming and Gardening with the Moon

As the moon wanes after the 5th, clip hair, trim hooves, worm livestock, prune shrubs or trees to retard growth and cut firewood. Plant your garlic, too.

Harvest honey from your hives (leaving plenty for the bees). Also bring in pumpkins and winter squash before the weather gets much colder.

Plants and bulbs intended for

spring forcing should be placed in light soil now and stored in a place where temperatures remain cool (but not freezing).

Although pasture growth may have stopped along the Canadian border, fields may be re-greening with secondary growth and fall varieties in many states south of the Great Lakes. Provide plenty of free choice hay to livestock in order to reduce the chance they will gorge themselves on fresh growth.

On the other hand, late pastures often contain less nutrition when soil temperatures drop near 40 degrees. Consequently, late-autumn feeding can be tricky; your animals may have plenty to eat, depending on the weather, but their grazing may give them less nutrition and energy than in the summer months.

The dark moon toward the end of the month favors vaccinations, surgery and livestock care. Since changes in the season bring weather extremes as well as stress, you will be taking care of routine health care at the most important time of the month and of the year.

As conditions permit, dig the tender gladiolus and dahlia bulbs in the North, and store them for the winter away from frost and moisture. In northern states, mulch root crops to keep them from turning to mush when the ground freezes solid. And all across the central states, you may want to heap leaves or straw around kale and collards in order to keep these hardy vegetables alive through numerous heavy frosts.

Gradually increase the feed to your livestock as the cold intensifies in order to provide them with sufficient autumn and winter energy.

As grazing season ends, gradually move your animals to supplements and hay. Avoid too many sudden changes in diet which can cause problems with both does and bucks. Plan to make a gradual feeding transition from Daylight Saving Time to Standard Time.

After the leaves come down from each of your trees, provide fertilizer that will gradually feed their roots through the late fall and winter.

The Moon and the Weather

Weather history indicates that cold waves will cross the Mississippi around the dates listed below.

The period between the 19th

through the 25th of the month brings an increased chance for dangerous weather, especially in the South. Full moon on October 5, perigee on October 9 and new moon on October 29 are likely to intensify weather systems near those dates.

October 2

The likelihood of frost becomes greater as October progresses, and the October 2nd front often combines with another front a day or two later to double the risk to tender pasture and garden plants. Chances for a hard freeze following this front are about ten percent at average elevations on the 40th Parallel. Along the Canadian border, expect light frost for sure. The full moon on October 5th may complicate travel and harvest with precipitation and wind.

October 7

Average temperatures have plunged six degrees throughout the country since September. Skies remain generally clear, but the afternoons are almost always cool. Full moon on October 5, along with lunar perigee on October 9, are likely to make the days and nights even chillier than average. The days after this front are often favorable for harvest, but precipitation increases (along with the chances for storms and snow in the North) as the

October 13th system approaches.

October 13

The coldest morning so far in the season often occurs as this front arrives, and chances of a low in the teens or 20s reach 20 percent in the northern half of the country for the first time since spring. This front often is the first front to bring a serious chance of snow flurries at average elevations along the 40th parallel. Highs below 50 degrees now occur about 30 percent of the time in the upper half of the United States.

October 17

After the passage of this front, the average amount of cloud cover increases markedly over that of last week, clouds being twice as likely to occur than in the first half of the month. Clouds mean slower drying time for hay and wool, not to mention an increase in seasonal stress. New moon on the 19th is expected to add cold to the clouds

October 23

Along the 40th Parallel, afternoon temperatures in the 50s and 60s usually accompany this front, and cold days only in the 30s or 40s occur one year in five. One year in three brings frost with this front everywhere above the Border States.

The period between the 23rd and the 31st, however, is often one of the mildest and driest times of autumn, and lunar apogee on the 24th increase the chances for good weather.

October 30

After this weather system comes across the country, milder but rainier weather typically follows for the first few days of November. The moon's weak position at the end of this October augurs well for Halloween activities.

Almanack Phenology: When... Then

When Halloween crops have come to town, then the dark-eyed juncos return to your bird feeders,

When you see streaks of scarlet in the oaks and shades of pink on the dogwood trees, then cut your gourds, winter squash and pumpkins for winter storage. Harvest your grapes, too.

When you see the fruits of the ginkgo tree turning pink, then look for next year's skunk cabbage in the swamp and the knuckles of next year's rhubarb in the garden.

When beggartick seeds stick to your pants legs, then check your horse for horse-bot eggs.

When the winged seeds of Japanese knotweed fall, then look for great flocks of blackbirds to move across the land.

When leaves reach peak color, that's the time to plant your winter wheat. That's also the time during which mating season begins for the white-tailed deer.

When ash leaves fall, then divide peonies, lilies and iris.

When maple leaves are down, then plant crocus, daffodils, tulips, snowdrops and aconites before November turns the weather much chillier.

When you see the pointers of the Big Dipper aligned north and south at 10:00 p.m., then dig your dahlias, gladiolus and cama bulbs for winter.

When the barn swallows leave your barn, begin the sugar beet harvest and look for frost within two weeks.

When the soft heads of cattails start to break apart, then complete autumn pruning of trees and shrubs.

When the first killing frost takes the peppers and tomatoes, then dig up the onions, remove the mum tops, cut flowers and herbs for drying.

When asparagus yellows in the garden, then transplant roses, pussy willows and perennials.

When you see the second bloom of forsythia bushes, then plan on about fourteen mild, dry days for outdoor work before winter.

After all the wheat and corn are harvested, then wrap new trees with burlap to help them ward off cold winds.

Peak Activity Times for Creatures

The following guide to lunar position shows when the moon is above (Best times) or below (Second-best times) the country, and, therefore, the period during which livestock, people, fish and game are typically the most active and the hungriest.

Date	Best	Second-Best
October 1 – 4:	Evenings	Mornings
October 5 – 11:	Midnight to Dawn	Afternoons
October 12 – 18:	Mornings	Evenings
October 19 – 26:	Afternoons	Midnight to Dawn
October 27 – 31:	Evenings	Mornings

Almanack Literature
Moe's Presents
By Pliny Fulkner
Hard Luck Farm, West Virginia

I have a cat named Moe, and he sleeps with me. He also likes to play with toy mice, the kind that are hollow and that you can fill with catnip.

Sometimes, after he plays with the toy mice, he sets them in his food dish. This seems to be some kind of offering to the food god, or a way of suggesting that something really needs to fill up that dish.

Sometimes, Moe brings the toy mice into my bed, and I wake up with a toy mouse on my pillow. It's usually not soggy, but it really doesn't belong on my pillow.

Moe also likes real live mice, and when he discovers one, he plays with it the way he plays with his toy mice. Maybe you can guess where this is going.

One night, Moe jumped up onto the bed as usual and went to sleep on my chest. We had a good sleep until we both heard a noise out in the hall. Zoom, and Moe was off to see what that noise was all about, but I dozed off.

I woke up again to Moe pouncing and jumping all over the covers. I sat up and then something wet struck me in the face and then I felt something get under the covers with me and it wasn't Moe. Then it was Moe, going after whatever had hit me and escaped into the bedding.

The sheet and blanket went flying. The cat went flying. A toy mouse went flying. I turned on the light. The mouse, sitting up on his haunches like a kangaroo ready to do battle, just waited for the next round.

Not up for more shenanigans, I

poured out the water from the glass that I had on my bedside table, scooped up the pugnacious mouse and put him outside.
I put Moe out, too.

NOVEMBER
2017

But let the months go round, a few short months,
And all shall be restored. These naked shoots
Barren as lances, among which the wind
Makes wintry music, sighing as it goes,
Shall put their graceful foliage on again,
And more aspiring and with ampler spread
Shall boast new charms, and more than they have lost.

William Cowper

The Gregorian Calendar
for November

S	M	T	W	T	F	S
			1	2	3	4
5	6	7	8	9	10	11
12	13	14	15	16	17	18
19	20	21	22	23	24	25
26	27	28	29	30		

Finding the Practice

I have been bringing together all my almanack notes, and it is becoming clearer to me that these notes are autobiographical, even though they seem to have little to do with me and everything to do with what is happening in nature at certain times throughout the small world in which I live.

I am finding that events which supposedly take place outside me are actually internal events. If external reality, as Einstein asserted, is altered by observation, how much more is the observer's reality altered by observing and by the internalizing of external events.

Anyone who stays in a house or town or relationship for an extended period of time undergoes this change. Since both observer and observed, subject and object, are completely porous, association, over time, permeates body and spirit.

Certain pieces of land or a garden or furniture take on lives of their own inside the one who lives with them. They grow into the self and resist exorcism, persist in memory and affect and flesh.

And so the hundreds of thousands of words I have collected in my daybook for the year, seep into me and out of me, and they are both the walk and the talk.

They are not unlike the objects in my house and yard with which I live and which are mnemonic and charged with story. They are not unlike the unwritten pieces of my life that shape my consciousness and unconsciousness, except that they are words that have shape and take up space in black and white.

I struggle with the banality in all this. I want to see meaning in larger, heroic terms, in pivotal decisions, in wrenching or joyful, life-changing incidents, and not in old chairs or a woman's glove or notes about the time a cardinal sang twenty-three years ago.

But as I go over and over all my notes, sometimes things come together. I see that the smallest things are enough, and that really they are everything.

The Apple Cider Moon and the Paperwhite Moon

As the leaves come down, apple cider time comes to a close, and toads and frogs complete migration, burrow down against the cold to come. Throughout the country, people set paperwhite and amaryllis bulbs in shallow water for holiday blooms.

November 4: The Deer Mating Moon is full at 12:23 a.m.
November 6: Lunar perigee (when the moon is closest to Earth)
November 10: The moon enters its final

quarter at 3:36 p.m.

November 18: The Paperwhite Moon is new at 6:42 a.m.

November 21: Lunar apogee (when the moon is farthest from Earth)

November 26: The moon enters its second phase at 12:03 p.m.

The S.A.D. Stress Index

The average length of November's night is almost as great as the night's length in December and January; the weather becomes more severe, and clouds thicken. S.A.D. increases to winter levels.

Key for Interpreting the S.A.D. Index:
Totals of 75 to 65: S.A.D. Alert: Severe Stress for those who suffer from seasonal affective disorders
64 to 50: Severe to moderate stress
49 to 35: Moderate stress
34 to 25: Light to moderate stress
24 and below: Low stress

Day	Clouds	Weather	Daylight	Totals
November 1:	13	17	22	52
November 15:	16	18	23	57
November 30:	19	19	24	62

The Sun

On November 23, the Sun enters the early winter sign of Sagittarius and reaches within two degrees of solstice at the same time. At the end of November, sunset has reached to within just a few minutes of its earliest time throughout the nation. The latest sunrise, however, is still about half an hour away.

Daylight Saving Time ends at 2:00 a.m. on Sunday, November 5. Set clocks back one hour at 2:00 a.m.

The Planets

Now in Libra, Venus reaches conjunction with Jupiter on the 13th (the best Venus-Jupiter display of the year), and it hugs the eastern horizon before sunrise until the middle of the month, when its brilliance is overcome by the sun. Mars in Virgo is the red morning star, higher than both Venus and Jupiter. Saturn becomes more and more difficult to see as it rides Ophiuchus into the sunset.

The Stars

An hour before sunrise, Regulus, centered overhead, announces the first bloom of violet cress and the full bloom of crocus. June's Arcturus is well up in the east. Warm Spica lies along the horizon. The Corona Borealis, the crown of peonies and iris and lily-of-the-valley, rises nearby. Vega has come full circle, is guiding Deneb and the Swan back from the northeast.

The seasons are as simple as day and night. The morning sky is always four months ahead of the evening sky. Eight hours after you see Orion looming up to foretell winter, he has gone. In four hundred eighty minutes, eight hours, the stars have moved one hundred twenty days, well past the flowering of aconites and red maples, almost to daffodils.

The Shooting Stars

Obscured by the full moon, the Taurid shower brings only a handful of meteors per hour on the 4th and 5th, but the Leonids (at the rate of about 15 per hour) should be more rewarding. Watch for them after midnight on the 17th and 18th. The dark moon will favor viewing of the Leonids this year.

Calendar of Feast Days and Holidays for Farmers, Gardeners and Homesteaders

November 23, 2017: Thanksgiving

Farming and Gardening with the Moon

The last bulb planting (including the garlic crop) and perennial transplanting should be done in anticipation of the arrival of the cold before full moon on the 4th. Around the yard, stake young shrubs and trees. Parsley and thyme should be brought inside in pots for winter seasonings. Wrap young transplants to protect them against frost cracking.

Routine care of your livestock may be less stressful to you and your animals if you take care of those activities in the first half of the month before the more severe cold waves arrive (and especially before new moon on the 18th).

All breeding of sheep and goats for next year's Easter market should now be complete. As November deepens, be sure the water is warm to encourage pregnant ewes and does to drink as much as they want.

The period of November 1 through 7 is often the driest time of the month. Transplant perennials, shrubs and trees. Cut your wood, fit storm windows, gather wild flowers for winter bouquets, and harvest corn and soybeans before the late autumn rains begin, often around the 8th of the month.

In the South, consider planting green manure cover crops between cold fronts as the moon waxes. Order your seeds and schedule your frost seeding for January and February, the time that the dramatic thaws of early spring can occur well into the North.

Cover round bales of hay with heavy tarps before the late fall rains and snows intensify. It's also time to keep an eye out for pneumonia in your animals. Maintain good ventilation (but no drafts) in the barn, and watch for stress from overcrowding.

The Moon and the Weather

Weather history indicates that cold waves will cross the Mississippi around the dates listed below.

If major storms do occur, weather patterns suggest that they will happen in the following periods: November 2 – 5, 14 – 16 and November 22 – 27. November 4 and 6 (full moon combined with perigee) and November 18 (new moon) are expected to increase the odds for cold and snow.

November 2

The first front of November is ordinarily one of the milder systems of the month, but this year's full moon on the 4th is likely to put a quick end to gentle weather. Perigee on the 6th doubles the chances for cold.

November 6

The November 6th front typically sharpens the divide between middle and late autumn, bringing much harsher conditions to states above the Mason-Dixon Line. As the percentage of cloud cover increases, winds gradually reach their winter levels, and full moon on the 4th and lunar perigee on the 6th will chill those winds.

November 11

Sun often follows this front and may provide some of the best days in the first half of the month for harvest. And if a killing frost has not occurred yet in the lower Midwest and in the Appalachians, the morning following this front may be the one to put an end to tender plantings.

November 16

As this front approaches, expect milder conditions, but an increased chance for precipitation. After the front moves through, favorable harvest conditions typically follow. New moon on the 18th will increase the chances for snow in the North and for tornadoes in the South.

November 20

The fifth major high to cross the nation in November usually begins to complicate the holiday travel season, and the chances for deep snow increase above the Border States. Like all the fronts of

November and December, this one pushes the hard-freeze line well into the South. Apogee on the 21st, however, does increase the chances for milder conditions.

November 24

This year the November 24th front coincides with a weak moon (entering its fourth phase and close to apogee), a coincidence that suggests this second-last front of the month could be less disruptive than usual during the Thanksgiving period.

November 28

The last cold front of November is almost always strong, and it typically brings rain and gloom to the South and snow to the North. It also brings a strong chance of freezing temperatures into the Gulf States and the Carolinas.

Almanack Phenology: When...Then

When all the mums are past their best, then major bird migrations will soon be over for the year.

When the yellow witch hazel still blooms, gardeners put in spring bulbs and dormant roses, and mulch perennials.

When thimbleweed heads are tufted

like cotton, then late fall arrives with killing frosts. That's the time to plan marketing goat and sheep cheese, Christmas cacti, dried flowers and grasses, poinsettias, mistletoe and ginseng for the holidays.

When Christmas cacti start to bud, then climbing bittersweet opens in the woods and almost every junco has arrived for winter.

The budding of Christmas cacti is also a sign that you should plant your amaryllis and paperwhite bulbs for January blooms.

When autumn violets end their season beside the woodland paths, then strawberries can be mulched with straw and peonies divided and transplanted.

When all the leaves are down, then fertilize trees and shrubs and remove tops from everbearing raspberries.

As mock orange and forsythia foliage thins, it measures the advance of winter. When all their leaves are down, a killing frost has occurred even in the mildest autumns.

When deer rutting season reaches its peak, then pastures are normally dormant.

When the poinsettia crop arrives at the market, then the last crickets die in the cold and many farmers are feeding hay to their livestock.

When beech and pear leaves finally fall, then early winter is only two weeks away.

Peak Activity Times for Creatures

The following guide to lunar position shows when the moon is above (Best times) or below (Second-best times) the country, and, therefore, the period during which livestock, people, fish and game are typically the most active and the hungriest.

Date	Best	Second-Best
November 1 – 3:	Evenings	Mornings
November 4 – 9:	Midnight to Dawn	Afternoons
November 10 – 17:	Mornings	Evenings
November 18 – 25:	Afternoons	Midnight to Dawn
November 26 – 30:	Evenings	Mornings

Almanack Literature
"We've Come A Long Way..."
by Vickie Wagner, Delta, Ohio

"Aunt Lottie is coming!" cried six-year-old Betty VanDyke.

Her mother, May, was busy preparing extra food. It was a special occasion when Aunt Lottie came to visit her brother, Klint VanDyke, on his farm near Delta, Ohio. All the VanDykes who lived in the area were invited to the farm to spend the day.

In the 1930s, the farm did not yet have the luxury of electricity or indoor plumbing. To Aunt Lottie, who lived in Grand Rapids, Michigan, this seemed old-fashioned. Almost as old-fashioned as the attitude that it wasn't proper for a lady to smoke cigarettes.

But Lottie respected her family: she would not smoke openly in their presence. She tried to hide her habit by escaping to the outhouse. She fooled no one, however, because streams of smoke always curled through the cracks in the privy walls when she was inside.

Six-year-old Betty and her young cousins thought it hilarious that Aunt Lottie really thought she was getting away with something. Brother Klint thought it funny, too; he would chuckle to the rest of the family: "Don't let Lottie know that we know that she smokes!"

No one ever did. And it became a family tradition to wait for her to make a trip to the outhouse and watch the smoke drift out into the country air.

DECEMBER 2017

Love to daily uses wed
Shall be sweetly perfected.
Life by repetition grows
Unto its appointed close:
Day to day fulfills one year.

Francis Thompson

The Gregorian Calendar for December

S	M	T	W	T	F	S
					1	2
3	4	5	6	7	8	9
10	11	12	13	14	15	16
17	18	19	20	21	22	23
24	25	26	27	28	29	30
31						

The Magic of Christmas

I am a child of Earth and Starry Heaven,
But my race is of Heaven alone.

Orphic Verse from the Petelia Tablets

Christmas approaches, and I get ready to go through the traditional practices of selecting and wrapping gifts, setting up the tree, helping to decorate the house. The first candle of the Advent wreath is burning as I write. Like many Christians, I wait for the rebirth of God and the land.

The natural year has put a clear end to the last leaves, garden greens and flowers. The nights are the longest of the year, and the days are gray. The sun lies at its cold solstice declination.

Evenings by the fire, I have been reading about the ancient Orphics, pre-Socratic Greeks whose ceremonies contained secret rituals that guaranteed safe passage to everlasting life. I have been reading about Dionysus, who died and rose again, and about Diana of the Ephesians, virgin earth goddess, distant antecedent of the Virgin Mary.

Many Sunday mornings, I attend mass. One of my favorite verses urges the congregation to come and take the body and blood of the Lord, the food and drink of immortality. I eat and drink, and I give in to all the rites of the season.

Still, I am always uneasy at this time of year, especially vulnerable to phobias and doubts. Who can tell if the sun will really move higher in the sky after solstice? Who can know for certain that Earth will really tilt back toward spring? Who really knows if I am immortal?

Like the Orphics, I am afraid and

need a secret formula. Bypassing the cerebral cortex, my heart and limbic sense tell me I had better place my bets on liturgy and mystery. In winter, the outside world is so indifferent. I build up the fire in my wood stove. Would-be child of Earth and Starry Heaven, I indulge in reckless magic and faith in Heaven alone.

The Paperwhite Moon and the Bedding Plant Moon

Among the various traditions that punctuate the darkest days of the year, the planting of paperwhites and amaryllis bulbs for bloom near winter solstice offers a modest transition into the next phase of the garden year, the seeding of bedding plants for May.

December 3: The Paperwhite Moon is full at 10:47 a.m. and reaches perigee, its position closest to Earth, today, as well. This is the only "Supermoon" (full at perigee) of 2017.

December 10: The moon enters its final quarter at 2:51 a.m.

December 18: The Bedding Plant Moon is new at 1:30 a.m. and at apogee (when it is farthest from Earth).

December 26: The moon enters its second phase at 4:20 a.m.

The S.A.D. Stress Index

The short day, the increase in cloud cover, and the growing cold all combine to produce high S.A.D. Index readings and, correspondingly, a high frequency of S.A.D. in humans.

Totals of 75 to 65: S.A.D. Alert: Severe Stress for those who suffer from seasonal affective disorders
64 to 50: Severe to moderate stress
49 to 35: Moderate stress
34 to 25: Light to moderate stress
24 and below: Light stress

Day	Clouds	Weather	Daylight	Totals
December 1:	19	19	24	62
December 15:	23	22	25	70
December 31:	24	23	25	72

The Sun

Winter solstice occurs at 11:28 a.m. on December 21. The Sun enters the deep winter constellation of Capricorn on the same day.

On the 24th the Sun begins its movements toward summer solstice, rising just slightly from the declination of 23 degrees, 26 minutes to 23 degrees, 25 minutes. (There are 60 minutes in a degree.)

On Christmas, it moves another minute. On the 26th, it rises a full two minutes, and then its ascent takes on greater and greater momentum, changing more than five minutes in a day by January 1, about ten minutes in a day by January 15, up to 20 minutes a day by February 1.

The Planets

♃ ♄ ♂ ♀

Venus and Saturn in Ophiuchus are not visible this month. Mars, moving retrograde into Libra, lies low on the eastern horizon with Jupiter before dawn.

The Stars

Orion looms in the east a few hours after dark; the three bright jewels of his belt are, from left to right, Alnitak, Alnilam, and Mintaka. Huge Rigel marks the right foot (that is on the right side) of Orion. Betelgeuse stands out to the upper left of his belt, as the raised arm of the giant.

An hour before sunrise, Orion has set. Sirius has moved deep into the west, Cancer and Gemini following it. The Big Dipper is overhead. June's Arcturus is coming in from the east, and August's Vega has come up in the northeast.

The Shooting Stars

The Ursid Meteors fall after midnight at the rate of about five to ten per hour on December 21 and 22. The young moon will favor your search for these shooting stars.

Calendar of Feast Days and Holidays for Gardeners, Farmers and Homesteaders

December 1, 2017: Muhammad's Birthday (Mawlid Al-Nabi): Sunni Muslims celebrate Muhammad's birthday today.

December 6, 2017: Muhammad's Birthday (Mawlid Al-Nabi): Shia Muslims celebrate Muhammad's birthday on this date.

December 12 – 20, 2017: Hanukkah: Festival of Lights

December 25, 2017: Christmas: Milk-fed lambs and kids below 20 pounds are favored for this market.

Farming and Gardening with the Moon

Put in bedding plants in the North and spring gardens in the South as the moon waxes. Plant bulbs, shrubs and trees throughout the Border States after full moon.

Do your month's slaughtering as the moon wanes through its third and fourth quarter (but don't let the carcasses freeze).

Prune trees and shrubs before the moon turns new, the lunar pivot for fresh growth to begin.

Try to complete harvest of corn, soybeans and sugar beets before the arrival of early winter, which normally storms in with the second December front, bringing the first taste of snow to the Border States and often a major blizzard to the North.

Throughout the South, put in greens as the moon waxes, root crops, shrubs and trees as the moon wanes.

The full force of winter may bring livestock into the barn much more often. Avoid overcrowding in order to cut down on the possibility of pneumonia. And keep adequate ventilation in any closed area your animals use on a regular basis.

If you haven't already done so, treat for mites and lice when you bring animals in from the cold.

Heavy December snows may limit the number of mice coyotes can catch. Livestock may start looking better and better to the hungry predators just before the holidays.

The Moon and the Weather

Weather history indicates that cold waves will cross the Mississippi around the dates listed below.

Weather patterns suggest that storms are most likely to occur during the following periods: December 1 – 3, 24 –

26, 31 – January 1. Full moon and perigee on the 3rd and new moon on the 18th are likely to hasten wintry conditions.

December 3

The first high-pressure system of December is normally one of the less violent fronts of the month. This year, however, full moon and lunar perigee on the 3rd should bring a fierce arrival to early winter.

December 8

The high pressure system that typically arrives at the end of December's first week is a major pivot for severe weather throughout the states along the 40th Parallel. A secondary front often increases the assault on your homestead between the 11th and the 13th.

December 15

This cold wave can bring below-zero temperatures as far south as the Border States, and double-digit below-zero temperatures enter the realm of possibility in over half the states of the Union. In milder years, the period between the passage of this front and the arrival of the New Year's front, sometimes offers a "halcyon" period of relatively gentle weather (sometimes called the Halcyon Days).

December 20
Even though lunar apogee occurs on December 18, new moon on that date may strengthen this front and contribute to more snow at higher elevations.

December 25
The Christmas cold front is one of the most consistent highs of the entire year, bearing precipitation five years in ten. It is typically followed by some of the brightest days of December. Travel and transport of livestock is recommended as this weather system moves east but before the arrival of the New Year's front.

December 31
The last front of the calendar year is typically windy and wet. After this weather system passes through, the chill of deep winter, empowered by the first full moon and lunar perigee of 2018, grips the nation for the next six to twelve weeks.

❦❦❦❦❦❦❦❦❦❦❦❦❦❦❦

Almanack Phenology: When-Then
When the last milkweed seeds scatter along the roadsides, then sunset is the earliest of the year and Canadian geese arrive in Louisiana.

When you hear honking above you

in the night, get up and search the dark sky for sandhill cranes moving south.

When sandhill cranes leave the Midwest, then brown pelicans are nesting along the Gulf of Mexico and larch trees are turning color in Maine.

When the second flowering of forsythia has ended, then gull migrations are finished, too, completing almost all major bird migration activity through the nation's midsection for the year.

When harvest is complete in the fields, fertilize with organic matter, phosophorus and potassium to reduce soil compaction.

When early winter arrives just after the moon is new, then order legume seed for next year's winter pastures.

When crocus and snowdrop foliage pushes up through the mulch, then mistletoe will be visible high in the branches of woodlots across the South.

When hepatica blooms in December, then lore suggests that the following spring will be warm.

When the yellow leaves of the New England aster fall, then the pear leaves and the beech leaves (the last holdouts of the canopy) soon fall, too.

When beech leaves have all come down across the North, then mangoes are in full bloom throughout southern Florida, and Florida grapefruit will soon be ripe.

When the very last leaves have been

taken from the trees, then ducks have completed migration and below-zero lows remain a possibility in the northern tier of states until aconites and snowdrops bloom.

When great flocks of crows gather for the winter, then early spring is only ten weeks away

When camel-back crickets appear in your house at night, expect colder weather and mice to follow.

Some Markers for the Progress of Spring at Average Elevations on the 40th Parallel

December 6: In all but the southernmost states, this is often the last day for the chance of a high temperature above 70 until January 21st (and the January Thaw).

December 7: Almost every leaf has fallen. Early winter begins.

December 21: Winter solstice is today.

January 1: Deep winter begins - a six week period when high temperatures often stay below freezing and the most snow falls throughout the northern half of the country.

January 2: The Earth reaches perihelion, its position closest to the sun.

January 23: This is the average date of the January thaw.

January 26: Cardinals begin their spring mating songs, and deep winter ends.

January 27: Late winter, a three-week transition to early spring, begins.

January 28: Average temperatures start to rise one degree per week throughout the country.

January 30: The earliest robins and bluebirds cross the 40th Parallel.

February 1: Doves call after sunrise.

February 2: The first snowdrops could blossom in the sun all along the 40th Parallel.

February 14: Red-winged blackbirds arrive in the northern half of the United States.

February 17: Today is Cross-Quarter Day: The sun is now halfway to equinox.

February 18: Average date for the start of early spring, a six-week period that gradually brings the landscape to life.

February 27: Average temperatures now rise one degree every three days, a pattern that persists until the middle of summer.

March 4: Pussy willows are usually completely open below Chicago.

March 8: Daffodils bloom in the Lower Midwest.

March 20: Equinox in 2018 occurs at 8:15 a.m.

Peak Activity Times for Creatures

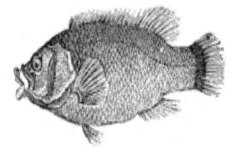

The following guide to lunar position shows when the moon is above (Best times) or below (Second-best times) the country, and, therefore, the period during which livestock, people, fish and game are typically the most active and the hungriest.

Date	Best	Second-Best
December 1 – 2:	Evenings	Mornings
December 3 – 9:	Midnight to Dawn	Afternoons
December 11 – 17:	Mornings	Evenings
December 18 – 25:	Afternoons	Midnight to Dawn
December 26 – 31:	Evenings	Mornings

Almanack Literature
Daria's Story
By Adrienne Barclay, Black Sheep Meadows, Waymart, Pennsylvania

When Daria arrived at Black Sheep Meadows with her mother last May, she was starving. At six weeks of age, she only weighed nine-and-a-half pounds, less than some of our newborn lambs. Her mother had given birth to twins but only had enough milk to feed her brother, so she had been abandoned.

The plan was to bring Daria's mother to the farm so that she would be able to feed her. We assumed that once we limited the competition from her brother, there would be plenty of milk. But her mother still rejected her, and Daria was again abandoned. She became our first bottle-fed baby.

We started by giving her a total of 10 mls a day divided into six bottles. In two months or so, she was up to eight ounces per bottle. We kept her separated in the house until she was strong enough to follow us down to the barn.

Whenever she went into the pasture, she was so small that she would completely disappear in the tall grass until we called her name. Then, she would suddenly appear out of nowhere and do her little sideways lamb dance all the way down to where we were standing, gladly accept her bottle and then return to the pasture.

So slow was her gain, however, that we decided that she would never grow to the size of the others and consequently could never become pregnant.

Then at first we didn't notice, but somewhere along the line, she started growing. Before we knew it, she was the size of the sheep in the rest of the flock, rambunctious as ever, but a much larger version. She would still come running when we called her name, but now she would butt her way to the front of the line to get that much coveted bowl of grains.

At 5:00 a.m. yesterday morning, she quietly gave birth to a beautiful, healthy ten-pound ram lamb. Daria, the little orphan who was rejected by her own mother had become a perfect and doting mother herself.

When ewes give birth, they have a special sound that they make when they are cleaning or caressing their little lambs. It is somewhere between a purr and a low growl, and can often be heard coming from lambing pens. Those contented sounds could be heard coming from Daria's pen all morning. We have come full circle, and the story is now, hopefully, complete.

Bill Felker

Valediction for the Year

Though under the snow,
just after solstice:
all of the fire of May
has been darkened,
deep in the South,
the cold starts to weaken
and loses momentum,
and winter and summer
are riding a fulcrum
as thin as a leaf,
and somewhere between
the marshes of Glynn
on the south coast of Georgia
and Everglades swamps,
somewhere between them
at peak of the tide,
the poles are reversing:
Instead of receding,
the warmth is returning,
and stirring the coals
far, far within,
of the distant, impossible
core of the spring.

Bill Felker

Bill Felker

An Almanacker's Autobiography
Bill Felker

My apprenticeship in almanacking began in 1972 with the gift of a barometer. My wife, Jeanie, gave the instrument to me when I was succumbing to graduate school stress in Knoxville, Tennessee, and it became not only an escape from intense academic work, but the first step on the road to a different kind of awareness about the world.

From the start, I was never content just to watch the barometric needle; I had to record its movement then graph it. I was fascinated by the alchemy of the charts, which turned rain and sun into visible patterns, symbols like notes on a sheet of music.

From my graphs of barometric pressure, I discovered that the number of cold fronts each month is more or less consistent, and that the earth breathes at an average rate of about once every three to five days in the winter, and once each six to eight days at the peak of summer.

Eventually, I learned when important changes would occur and what kind of weather would take place on most any day. That information was expressed in the language of odds and percentages, and it was surprisingly accurate. Taking into consideration the consistency of certain patterns in the past, I could make fairly successful predictions about the likelihood of the repetition of such patterns in the future. The pulse of the world was more steady than I had ever imagined.

My graphs also allowed me to see the special properties of each season. August's barometric configurations, for example, are slow and gentle like low, rolling hills. Heat waves show up as plateaus. Thunderstorms are sharp, shallow troughs in the gentle waves of the atmospheric landscape. Autumn arrives like the sudden appearance of a pyramid on a broad plain. By the end of September, the fronts are stronger; the high-pressure peaks become taller; the lows are deeper, with almost every valley bringing rain. By December, the systems loom on the horizon of the graph like a range of mountains with violent extremes of altitude, sometimes snow-capped, almost always imposing and sliced by canyons of wind.

From watching the weather, it was an easy step to watching wildflowers. Identifying plants, I saw that flowers were natural allies of my graphs, and that they were parallel measures of the seasons and the passage of time. I kept a list of when each wildflower blossomed and saw how each one consistently opened around a specific day, and that even though a cold year could set blooming back up to two weeks, and unusual warmth accelerate it, average dates were quite useful in establishing sequence of bloom that always showed me exactly where I was in the progress of the year.

In the summer of 1978, my wife and I took the family to Yellow Springs, Ohio, a small town just beyond the eastern edge of the Dayton suburbs. We bought a house and planned to stay. I began to write a nature column for the local newspaper. To my weather and wildflower notes I added comments on foliage changes, bird migration dates, farm and gardening cycles, and the rotation of the stars. The microclimate in which I immersed myself gradually became a key to the extended environment; the part unlocked the whole. My Yellow Springs gnomon that measured the movement of the sun along the ecliptic also measured my relationship to other places on earth.

My occasional trips turned into exercises in the measurement of variations in the landscape. When I drove 500 miles northwest, I not only entered a different space, but often a separate season, and I could mark the differences in degrees of flowers, insects, trees, and the development of the field crops. The most exciting trips were taken south in March; I could travel from early spring into middle spring and finally into late spring and summer along the Gulf Coast.

My engagement with the natural world, which began as an escape from school (and helped me stop smoking, as well), finally turned into a way of getting private bearings. It became a process of spiritual and physical reorientation. In that sense, all the seasonal notes in this book are the fruit of a strong need to define where I am, who I am and what happens around me. It is my hope that *Poor Will's Almanack* will help you to find your own seasons and place, as well.

∽✦⫷⫷⊕ ⫷⫷⫷🜉 ⫷⫷⊕ ⫷⫷⊕ ⫷⫷∼

Bill Felker has been writing *Poor Will's Almanack* for papers and magazines since 1984, and he has published annual almanacks since 2003. His radio version of *Poor Will* is broadcast weekly on NPR station WYSO and is available on podcast.

For more information, visit Bill Felker's phenology website at www.poorwillsalmanack.com

.